Putting Together the Entrepreneurial Puzzle

Putting Together the Entrepreneurial Puzzle

The Ten Pieces Every Business Needs to Succeed

Mary E. Marshall

Veritas Vincit Press

VERITAS VINCIT PRESS
Putting Together the Entrepreneurial Puzzle:
The Ten Pieces Every BusinessNeeds to Succeed

Editor: Monica Payson
Cover Design: Ana Grigoriou
Interior Design: Monica Payson
Indexer: D'Ann Hamilton-White
Author Photo: Tara Gimmer

Published in the United States by Veritas Vincit Press
ISBN 978-0-9913650-0-5

For my boys, Chris and Andrew: the best products I ever took to market.

Contents

Foreword

As a global futurist, I see persistent anemic job creation across every marketplace in our global economy. This is not a puzzle we can't solve, but the future won't resemble the past when most "good jobs" were created by big business. Instead, our current conundrum will be solved by small businesses. And that's why we must invest in helping entrepreneurs design and profitably grow their companies.

Small business in America creates around fifty percent of new jobs. Yet CEOs across every industry face challenges in growing their companies beyond the $1 million revenue mark. I've wanted to forecast that small business would grow significantly over the next ten to twenty years and become the engine of growth, but I couldn't find enough evidence to support that forecast. Intrigued, I launched my own research to investigate what prevents entrepreneurs from growing their businesses. After seven years of working with a diverse group of CEOs, I've come to some conclusions and I believe *Putting Together the Entrepreneurial Puzzle: The Ten Pieces Every Business Needs to Succeed* provides a key to making my forecast a reality.

During my research I had the good fortune of meeting Mary E. Marshall, a successful CEO and a seasoned, sought-after executive coach in the northwestern U.S. Up until now the lack of an effective guide to the hazard-filled enterprise of growing a small business has been a fundamental impediment to small business success. Mary E. Marshall's excellent book *Putting Together the Entrepreneurial Puzzle* fills that gap with an accessible, practical, clear compendium of tools and knowledge every busy CEO can easily use to move from entrepreneur to business person, from the excitement of startup into the tough reality of maturing a successful business. By focusing on the ten critical areas that hamstring most businesses this stellar guide will become an essential tool for every CEO of a small business.

Putting Together the Entrepreneurial Puzzle is aimed at solving the thorniest issues that cause small businesses to fail. With my early access to the book I was able to use several of the ideas and tools with my group of CEOs. These tools work. Not only does Mary provide guidance for CEOs to become proficient at business basics—vision, mission, and values as well as financial metrics—but she also provides essential tools for addressing issues that are seldom focused on including marketing. While most CEOs are great at sales (an essential skill during startup) their poor marketing capabilities result in chronic under performance. Understanding the essential framework of a marketing plan and the need for a strong team will help CEOs delegate this task strategically at any stage of business growth. Indeed one of the most important themes that runs through all of the practical as well as the more theoretical chapters is effective leadership.

At the beginning of the twenty-first century we left behind years of strong job growth, rising incomes, and broad-based prosperity in America. The return to such a market will ride to a large extent on our ability to create robust growth of many more small businesses. Mary E. Marshall's gift of a book will help your business become part of that future growth. Get one for every CEO you know!

Mary O'Hara-Devereaux, Ph.D.
    CEO, Global Foresight
    Finding Targets No One Else Can See
    San Francisco, California
Author of *Navigating the Badlands:*
    Thriving in the Radical Decade of Transformation

A Note of Thanks

There are many people I need to thank for helping to make *Putting Together the Entrepreneurial Puzzle* a reality. First, all the entrepreneurs I've worked with and whose stories I've shared. You inspired me to write this book and have informed my beliefs about what makes a successful entrepreneur. It's been terrific to be a part of your journey and learn from you. You each have a place in my heart. This book is dedicated to each of you and all those many entrepreneurs to come after you!

To my friends and family who supported me through this project, thank you. Your encouragement has been amazing and this book would not have been the same without you. In particular I want to thank my two sons, Chris and Andrew, who in their own ways are entrepreneurs in the making and who have allowed me to test out some of my theories on them.

I also want to thank all the organizations that very generously allowed me to reprint their materials in this book: the American Society of Training and Development (ASTD), Conversant, RealTimeCEO, RecruitLoop, The Richmond Group, and Stonetrust Commercial Insurance Company.

Lastly, I want to thank Monica Payson (Emdash Editing), my editor, and Donna Frindt, my book production project management guru, for all their help and inspiration as I would never have made it through this process without these two amazing ladies.

Introduction

Throughout my career as a business owner, leader, and CEO coach, I've had the privilege to work with entrepreneurs at various stages of their companies' growth cycles. Over the years, I've wondered why some leaders make it through the gauntlet of entrepreneurship and others don't. Why do some MBAs fail while the mom next door working from her kitchen succeeds? All too often I've seen that both success and failure come as a complete surprise. Is there a secret to solving the entrepreneurial puzzle? I think there is, and that's why I've written this book.

Entrepreneurial businesses make up seventy percent of the U.S. workforce, and their CEOs come to their positions in a variety of ways. Some purchase a business, some start a business from scratch, still others inherit the family business. Some of these entrepreneurs end up running their own businesses because their basic temperament just doesn't allow them to work for or take direction from anyone else. Most people who start or purchase their own business do so because they're idea people and they have a passion for a particular vision. They may have a high degree of competency in one area, but few are trained in or even familiar with all facets of entrepreneurship, in particular the nuts and bolts of managing the business.

Even if you've come to your position with an MBA, you're not likely to have all the pieces you need to solve the puzzle of running an entrepreneurial business. Like most people in your position, you've probably done much if not most of your learning "on the job." While that knowledge has certainly served you well, you've probably felt that there are some aspects of your business that are not running as smoothly as you'd like, or even that the total picture is murkier than it should be. This book is designed to give you the essential pieces of running a business so you can successfully guide yours through the entrepreneurial journey.

My goal in writing this book is to help you avoid the bruises and pitfalls I've witnessed with CEOs who ignored the fact that the skill or leadership gaps they don't acknowledge have an undeniable and significant negative impact on their companies. You may have one employee or 5,000, but ultimately you are responsible for what happens in your business. This book can help you gain the skills you need to take charge and make success happen. Whether you call yourself CEO or not, if you own and run a business you are the Chief Executive Officer and the buck stops with you. So embrace your role and start taking charge of your business!

Putting Together the Entrepreneurial Puzzle: The Ten Pieces Every Business Needs to Succeed is the result of my work with CEOs who took a deliberate approach to their businesses: they were intentional about culture, values, and vision; they clarified their roles; and they learned the secrets of hiring well so their teams made their businesses grow. Because of this intentional approach, their businesses were more successful than their competitors. In other words, they succeeded where their peers did not because they understood and put together more pieces of the entrepreneurial puzzle. I wrote this book because I've learned that the more pieces of the entrepreneurial puzzle you have, the more successful your business will be.

Most entrepreneurs have shelves (or nightstands or desks) full of books on the different aspects of running a business. Each one of those books is aimed at solving a discrete piece of the puzzle. You probably have some of those books. Maybe you've even read some of them. But my guess is that none of those books solved the problem you hoped they would solve because they didn't give you a holistic way of looking at your enterprise. *Putting Together the Entrepreneurial Puzzle* gives you the ten basic pieces of the puzzle in one place as a reference guide to grow and run your business.

Think of this book as your entrepreneurial owner's manual. It's the place to look when something in your business gets stuck, but it's also the place to look to get a comprehensive overview of how to keep your business running well.

The temptation with a book like this is to jump right to the section that seems to address the issue that is most obvious to you now. Although you can certainly look for the puzzle piece that helps you solve an immediate problem, I hope you'll continue all the way through. I know you're busy. And I know you're eager to get down to business. But the skills in this book build on one another, and moving through them sequentially will help you create a new way of thinking about your company. Each chapter has a checklist and resources at the end that will help you relate what you've just learned to what is happening in your company, and deepen your knowledge on the topic if you choose. As your confidence increases that you know what to do and how to do it, you'll see results in all areas of your business.

My wish for you as you apply what you learn in this book is that you develop productive employees who are aligned with your vision and values, that you attract happy customers, and that you make lots of money and have fun along the way.

Puzzle Piece One
Intentional Purpose

We've all seen mission, vision, and values statements on lobby walls, in marketing material, or on websites. They're usually well crafted, and are meant to convey the best intentions of the owners or the employees (hopefully both) so others understand what the company is all about. But how often do these statements achieve genuine understanding and trust between a business and its customers?

Most businesses go through the motions of creating mission, vision, and values statements. In many cases, those statements are forgotten almost as soon as they're written. Everyone is glad the assignment is over so they can get on with their real work. And, while they might have believed all the words they crafted, no one sat down to actually think through how those concepts would be lived in the company on a daily basis. Perhaps they *don't* get lived in the company. Or, perhaps at some point in the company's evolution, its mission, vision, or values changed so that its daily activities are no longer in sync with its stated values. Incongruities like these are felt by your employees as well as your customers.

Most of the statements I encounter leave me wondering what the CEO (or committee, or marketing team, or whoever was tasked with writing the statements) was thinking, because the words aren't in keeping with what I see in the lobby, the marketing materials, or online. In other words, the words don't feel authentic in the context of my actual experience. For example, a statement declaring that Joe's Accounting is dedicated to the customer falls flat when I'm left waiting in the lobby for ten minutes before even being greeted.

Clarifying your mission, vision, and values isn't just one of those assignments you have to get through so you can get on with business. Your mission, vision, and values *are* your business. Using the puzzle metaphor for creating or jumpstarting a business enterprise, think of these three concepts as the edge and corner pieces of the puzzle. Mission and vision are the framework for your business, because, without them, it's almost impossible to complete the rest of the picture, and what you do put together will be rough and unbalanced. Values are the corner pieces because they keep your enterprise true, in all senses of the word.

Understanding Mission, Vision, and Values

You've probably seen various descriptions for these three words. I suspect they're some of the most overused terms in business, but also the least understood. Worse, although they're the subject of much discussion, even when they are articulated, they are rarely used as the guiding principles they're meant to be and even more rarely lived within a business's day to day culture. So let's start from scratch. Below are my definitions of "mission," "vision," and "values," followed by information and exercises on how to use them to run what I call an Intentional Business. These are the core concepts to clarify before you go any further. In other words, get the edges and corners of your puzzle in place and square before you try to figure out the rest of your entrepreneurial puzzle.

Mission usually answers the questions, Why are we here? and What do we stand for? Building from the answers to those questions, **Vision** is the future that will exist if you succeed in your mission. **Values** are the beliefs at the core of your business that act as a compass to guide behavior and decisions for *everyone* in the company. Let's delve into each of these pieces in a little more depth.

Mission

Successfully defining and pursuing your vision requires that you first understand the intention or purpose of your business. In other words: Why are you in business at all? What problem are you solving? What will be better or different as a result of your business being successful? In terms used by Dave Logan, author of *Tribal Leadership: Leveraging Natural Groups To Build A Thriving Organization*, what is your "Noble Cause?" Without a clear and compelling purpose, your business might survive, it might even be successful, but your progress will be accidental. Just think how hard it would be to build a car if you didn't know what the pile of parts was supposed to do when you were done. What are the odds you would build a functioning machine? So, as you read further, take some time to think hard about your mission. Ask yourself: if my business didn't exist, what would be missing in the world? What problem would not be solved? Who would not be served?

Vision

Growing out of a clear and intentional mission, your vision is not just a statement on the wall; it's the future everyone in your company is working toward. If your business were to succeed beyond your wildest expectations in its first year, what would that look like? What would years two and three look like?

Values

Vision questions are important, and, in some ways, they are the fun ones to ponder because they require you to imagine your company's success. However, before you can clearly define either your mission or your vision, you have to answer the most important question of all: what are your values? As the leader, what do *you* stand for? What are *your* core values? What principles was your company founded on? What are the intolerables in your business? There are no right or wrong answers to these questions because your values belong to you.

Defining Your Values

While values are often tagged on after mission and vision, as I've just said, it's important that you start your Intentional Purpose exercise by defining your values first. Values are the foundation of your business identity and they should inform all the decisions you make.

We all have values. They may not be stated, we may not even know what they are, but we have them. Sometimes they show up in our businesses, sometimes not. But they always show up in our behaviors. Think of your values as the framework on which your identity is built. We develop our values from our upbringing, our beliefs, our role models, and from our experiences in general. One way to start thinking intentionally about your values is to think of the key experiences in your life that inform who you are and the choices you make.

When I was sixteen I had one of those key, values shaping experiences. Shortly before returning from a year as an exchange student in Costa Rica, I learned that my father had abandoned our family of seven children. This alone was a terrible shock for a very close Catholic family, but I also learned that we had no money because my dad didn't leave any. The oldest daughter, I arrived home to find my home very different from when I had left. Suddenly my mom was working and in a fog, we were on welfare, the church was leaving food baskets on our doorstep, and my brothers and sisters were a mess.

One of the hardest losses for me was discovering that, in my absence, my room had been given to another sibling and my few belongings had been passed on to my sisters. I was told I would have a room that used to belong to my younger brother. You can imagine what it looked like. In a big family having something all your own is a rarity. Losing *all* of what had been mine at once hit hard.

After I had been home about a week, my grandfather came to visit. Looking around my room, he said, "This doesn't look like you. Would you like to change it?" Of course I said, yes. So my grandfather took me to the store where we picked out wallpaper and paint. For the next week he showed me how to transform my unwanted room into something beautiful. But more important than regaining a sense of space, was the quiet wisdom my grandfather imparted to me as we worked. He never said anything more negative about my father than, "I don't understand how a man can abandon his family." But he followed that with a key value that has become part of who I am: "It's important to always do the right thing, no matter the cost." The room my grandfather helped me make was wonderful, but the real gift was the lasting lesson of honor, integrity, and authenticity he taught me. What moments in your life have had that kind of lasting impact on who you are and how you make choices?

Another way to intentionally consider your values is to think about what Dave Logan refers to as "high five" and "hell no" moments. High five's are any experience that went amazingly well or resulted in great accomplishments. Ask yourself: what made those moments great? Why were they important? If you really analyze those moments, there's probably a value in there somewhere that made it significant for you. Hell no moments are those times when you refused to do something, or stood up for something, probably at great cost. Those moments are key because a value was being violated for you. What was it?

Before you move on to defining your mission (why you are here) and vision (where you want to be in X amount of time), give some serious thought to your values. Defining your values first is essential because they're what keep everything else in true. Most companies will have four to eight core values, and, if they're being intentional, they'll know exactly what they mean. Take the time to be really clear here because words can have nuances, and it's essential that everyone inside and outside of your company know *exactly* what you mean by your values statements.

Defining Your Intentional Mission

The importance of really clarifying your mission is that *everything* else flows from it. Consider your mission the foundation of your business: a shaky foundation produces a weak business. Once you know your mission, you can begin to ask and answer important strategic questions within that framework. For instance, imagine your business one year from now, and answer each of the following questions prefaced by the frame, "If I am in service of my mission …":

- What problem will I be solving?
- What difference will I have made through my company's success?
- Where will my company be located?

- How many customers will I have?
- What will my role in the company be?
- What will my organizational chart look like?
- How many employees will I have?
- What revenues and profits will I have generated?
- What strategic partnerships/ventures will I have made?
- What's next?

In formulating your mission statement, start by plugging it into the following formula (you can work on making it sound elegant once you've clarified the basic concepts): "We exist to do X, we do it for X, and we do it by X." One way to determine if you're on the right track is to talk about it with other people and watch for their reactions. If you get questions and they seem excited and interested, you're probably onto something. If they change the subject, you have a dud. Go back to square one.

Microsoft's mission was to put a computer in every home. That's an undeniably compelling purpose, and Microsoft largely succeeded. (They also made a lot of money along the way—intentional missions have a way of doing that.) Of course every business is not as glamorous as Microsoft, but any business can have a compelling mission. Here are a few examples of powerful intentional mission statements:

- Marriott Residence Inn: To provide our guests a home away from home.
- Pacific Theaters: To provide a place for people to flourish and to enhance the community.
- Mary Kay Cosmetics: To give unlimited opportunity to women.
- Aflac: To combine aggressive strategic marketing with quality products and services at competitive prices to provide the best insurance value for consumers.

What's your intentional mission?

Defining Your Intentional Vision

Your vision is the future you are making. It's where you want your company to be in a given time frame. Defining your intentional vision is about looking beyond the constraints of the present and seeing what *could* be. In developing your vision statement, try to complete this sentence: "A year from now, we will be …".

The CEO of a small accounting firm I worked with could not see a vision beyond one or two staff simply because that's the way it had always been. Not surprisingly, he didn't have a clear intention for what he wanted for his company. As it turned out, what he really wanted was to create a firm with fifty employees in five years. But, to discover that, we first had to focus on his true intention: Was it to create a certain size firm? Was it to service a certain type of customer? Was it to provide excellent advice to businesses so they made sound decisions and maximized their tax advantage? Once we had clarified *why* he was in business, he could get excited about what he was doing and the *where*, the vision, could begin to emerge from that.

As a next step I had him close his eyes and literally visualize his business: his desk, his office, the windows, the lobby, all the employees' desks, the customers. The first thing he needed to do was imaginatively move past the present reality in order to ask himself: "If it were *possible*, what would it look like?" Kids are experts at this kind of thinking, but as adults we inhibit our creative thinking by putting "can't happen filters" on possibility. The *New Oxford American Dictionary* defines vision as "[t]he ability to think about or plan the future with imagination or wisdom." Defining your vision, therefore, requires thinking outside of your current constraints. If money, time, and people were unlimited—if there were literally no resource constraints whatsoever—what would you create?

As soon as this CEO started thinking about what was possible, instead of what *wasn't* possible, he started to develop a clear picture of where he wanted to go. A year later, he had increased his staff to ten and was still growing. True entrepreneurs are defined by their belief in possibilities—just try to talk them out of it!

Once you have the picture of what your intentional vision looks like, just as you did with your mission, test it out on a few people. Tell them about it and listen to what they say, but also watch their body language and facial expressions. Don't get discouraged if they look at you like you've lost all common sense. Just sit back, listen, and ask questions. You need to be able to listen objectively so you can learn how to describe your vision in a way that creates enthusiasm and energy. This is also a good opportunity to make course corrections if necessary or to fine tune how you deliver your message. A good friend and colleague of mine teaches leaders how to speak about themselves and their companies. Her favorite phrase for getting people to tap into their own enthusiasm about a topic is to ask what "spins your jets" about it. So, in thinking about how to communicate your intentional vision, figure out what spins your jets about it and why. When you test your vision statement on others, pay attention to what spins their jets. Is the thing that gets them excited what you want them to get excited about?

After you've clarified your intentional vision, and others have validated that you sound credible when describing it, it's critical for everyone in your company to understand the vision and to decide whether or not they're on board. You want your whole company to be excited about the vision and committed to it. Everyone in the company is, by default, in sales (no matter what role they play in the organizational scheme), and if they don't believe in the intentional vision, they can't sell it. Talk about your vision early and often, and make sure everyone has the words to talk about it. If they can talk about it in their own words that's even better because then the vision means something to them personally. You want your business staffed by people who are excited about why your company exists and where it is going.

Who Needs to Know?

In addition to your employees, who else needs to know what your Intentional Purpose (your values, mission, and vision) is? *Everyone!* People want to associate themselves with people who know what they stand for (values), why they exist (mission), and where they are going (vision). Getting people excited about being associated with you starts with making sure that all of your employees, customers, and partners know what your Intentional Purpose is. Make sure it is clearly communicated by everything your company does. Getting your message across clearly and energetically will help your employees, customers, and partners tell others about your company. Make telling your story fun and easy for people and they will do it for you.

How is Your Company Living Its Intentional Purpose?

People look for congruency: do you actually walk the talk? This is where your values, and, as a result your behavior, tell more about you and your company than any statement. Most people have pretty good BS detectors, so make sure you know how your vision is being "lived" in your organization. Living your Intentional Purpose on a daily basis means creating systems and processes that are aligned with what you believe, who you are, and where you are headed. Use your Intentional Purpose as an overlay to all decisions made within your company. And if employees know this, just think how much easier it will be for them to make good decisions. The easier you make it for employees, customers, and partners to experience your Intentional Purpose on a regular basis, the more that purpose will become reality. As a leader, it's your job to create an environment that promotes the Intentional Purpose of your company every single day.

One CEO I worked with was revisiting his company's mission, vision, and values. He felt it was important to include the word "fun." When I questioned him about what the company did to fulfill the promise of "fun," his answer was that they held a summer picnic and a holiday party. I asked if having "fun" twice a year seemed like fun. He smiled and said, "Not really." Now, I don't mean that you shouldn't have fun implementing your Intentional Purpose. Just make sure that what you state as your purpose genuinely reflects what you are all about and what you want to achieve. In other words, your Intentional Purpose needs to be based, not on catchy slogans, but on a foundation of values that are true for you.

Now it's your turn to create your Intentional Purpose. Everything else in your business will flow from the work you do in this first chapter. It's important, so take as much time as you need. If you already have a mission or vision statement, can you remember it? Does it still make sense? Do you know the values it comes out of? Are you living it on a daily basis in your company? If not, start over. Values first.

Intentional Purpose Checklist

- ❐ Describe your company's values. List 4 to 8.
- ❐ Describe your company's mission: We exist to do X (what), we do it for Y (who), and we do it by Z (how).
- ❐ Describe your company's vision: A year from now we will be X.
- ❐ Describe how you will communicate this.
- ❐ List everyone you will tell about your Intentional Purpose.
- ❐ Describe how will you communicate your Intentional Purpose to everyone you have listed.
- ❐ Describe how you will live your Intentional Purpose.

Recommended Reading

The Corporate Mystic: A Guidebook for Visionaries with Their Feet on the Ground, Gay Hendricks and Kate Ludeman, Bantam, 1996.

Tribal Leadership: Leveraging Natural Groups to Build a Thriving Organization, Dave Logan, John King, and Halee Fischer-Wright, HarperBusiness, 2011.

Puzzle Piece Two
Intentional Culture

Why does culture matter? Whether it's intentional or not, every company has a culture. You can walk through the door and feel it almost the instant you step in. What does the lobby look like? What's on the walls? Is it warm or cool? Clean or shabby? Quiet or loud? How are you greeted? Even if you don't think you have a clearly defined culture in your company, you do. You may not be able to describe it, but I'll bet others can and do, to your competitors as well as to your potential customers.

Culture is the daily demonstration of a company's values. Culture can be the manifestation of stated values (intentional), or the unstated but nonetheless real values that some or all of the employees share, but that are unstated (unintentional). As we discussed in the last chapter, spending a lot of time on your Intentional Purpose (values, mission, and vision) will be a waste unless that truly translates into the *lived* culture of your organization. Make sure they match: Culture = Lived Values.

The risk of not being intentional about your company's culture was illustrated to me by an encounter I had with Peter Schutz of Porsche, when he came to speak to one of my TEC CEO groups about getting extraordinary results out of ordinary people. (The Executive Committee is now

Vistage International.) The meeting was held at a member's company, a software firm. As we were waiting for everyone to arrive, Peter approached me and said, "Come here, I want to show you something." We walked down the hall and he pointed out several offices. They were messy and chaotic, with lots of personal items on display. He asked me if I thought this company had trouble sticking to plans and meeting deadlines. My answer was an emphatic "Yes!" And, in fact, those were the biggest challenges the company faced. Those offices belonged to developers who were allowed enormous flexibility in their work schedules, but were not held accountable when they didn't meet deadlines.

The owner of this company is a brilliant thinker, inventor, and idea person. He didn't purposely set out to create a chaotic culture; it just happened as a result of his experimental personal style. While not fatal, this unintentional culture hampered his company's growth. The business was making it because they had a product no one else had, but they had plateaued at $5 million in revenue because the owner, and consequently his team, kept reinventing the product. Because they didn't have a culture of reasonable limits and accountability, the product was never good enough, and they continued to tinker until some clients grew frustrated and went elsewhere. Ultimately, the culture of unaccountability kept the company stuck, continuously repeating the same mistakes.

Unintended culture also presents significant problems with employees. First, without an intentional culture, it's hard to accurately identify why someone should work for you. You're left hiring based on skills alone, and skills by themselves don't speak to whether or not a person will fit in and manifest your company's values. An additional risk is that some of your employees will set the culture for you, and it's rarely your best employees who will do that. These people are like bullies on the playground: if the playground monitor isn't watching, they'll set the rules and tone that everyone has to play by. A third drawback is that, in the absence of intentional culture as a unifying force, employees will head in different directions, accomplishing their own tasks in their own ways. This lack of cohesion in the team ultimately leads to lack of results.

Have you really thought about your company's culture? Cultural confusion is more common than you might think, and a little examination should tell you if your company's culture is preventing you from attaining the success you'd like to have. Even though some aspects or departments of your company might have a pretty defined set of values and therefore a culture, it's essential that your *entire* company understand and live the same culture. No facet of your company can fully achieve its goals without the entire company adhering to the same culture. Nor can your company achieve its overall vision without everyone upholding that culture. Take a look at how your company functions: lack of communication, lack of follow through, misunderstandings, unmet deadlines, and low morale are all symptoms of a dysfunctional culture.

What Do You Want Your Culture to Be?

Patrick Lencioni, author of several books on culture and teams, describes a fictional company in his book *The Four Obsessions of an Extraordinary Executive: A Leadership Fable*. In this company, the owners have described their culture in three words: "Hungry, humble, and smart." They decided that anyone coming into the company needed to have drive (be hungry), needed to be respectful (be humble), and needed to be the best at what they do so they could think on their feet (be smart). The owners then looked at all their people to make sure everyone fit that culture, and they made changes with anyone who did not. They knew that one exception could take their company in a wrong direction, because one negative has more impact and influence than five positives. Next they evaluated all of their processes to make sure those too were hungry, humble, and smart. In doing all of this they also found that their best customers fit that description as well.

Although this process takes place in a fictional company, the same exercise works very well in real companies. I've given this assignment to CEOs, and, more often than not, the ones who can describe their culture in three words and identify those traits in their employees as well as in their company's processes are the most successful. They are the ones who continue to grow their businesses and make it look easy.

I've noticed a lot of firms adopting three words to describe themselves in marketing materials, and I've been curious about how that works inside the organization. Are those three words intentional culture or just a catchy tag line? A tag line is good for show (it looks great on marketing materials), but living the meaning of those words inside the organization as well as in your interactions with the outside world is what your company needs in order to grow. Make sure the words you choose reflect and describe your intentional culture. You can use any three words as long as you are very clear about what those words mean to you and your company. If you can't reduce it to three words, use four or five, but keep in mind that it's harder to create systems and processes that have more than three purposes. You might find it helpful to prioritize, and then pick the top three.

As with your mission and vision, identifying and implementing your company's culture is essential because your lived values will drive so many of your key decisions. We'll talk about this in more depth in Chapters Four and Five, but I'll give an example here to illustrate the importance of this. A financial services firm I worked with was having trouble recruiting and hiring a second-in-command to eventually replace the CEO. Instead of continuing to examine applicant skills, I had the CEO come up with three words to describe his company's culture. He decided that "accountable" (responsible for one's actions, reliable for results), "smart" (able to think independently and of above average intelligence), and "dedicated" (devoted to getting the best results for his clients) best described his company's intentional culture. Once he was able to define this, his vision about who that person was became clear and within three months he had located and hired the person who fit the position. Defining his company's culture so succinctly allowed him to successfully communicate his company's intentional purpose to a candidate, and identify those same traits in the person he ultimately hired. Just as this CEO used his three-word intentional culture statement to make hiring decisions, yours can act as an overlay to everything you and your employees do within your company.

Communicating Your Intentional Culture to Your Employees

If you're just starting a company, it's much easier to communicate your intentional culture to each new prospective recruit or employee. You can make it part of your employee handbook and orientation, and have it posted around the office in visible places. But, more than just the visuals, you need to live your values from the top down. The minute an employee sees you or the management team doing something counter to your stated values, game over. At that moment a new culture has been created and it's called, "Lack of Integrity." Remember the old saying that most people will give you their trust once for free, but you have to earn it back forever once it's broken? Well, the same goes for culture within your company.

One company CEO I worked with liked to think of himself as the "father," and he took excellent care of his employees, creating a very patriarchal culture. Then the company hit hard times. Suddenly people were laid off, salaries were frozen, and bonuses were eliminated. Yet the employees were expected to give the same level of performance if not more. What resulted was a bunch of petulant teenagers all rebelling because father didn't take care of them anymore. To this day that company's culture has never returned to father-knows-best, and, because of the breach of trust, it has never performed as well either. The patriarchal culture was replaced by an "it's not fair, distrust and entitlement" culture. The lesson here is that it doesn't matter what your culture is (assuming, of course, that it's legal and ethical) as long as you know what it is, you can articulate it inside and outside, and you believe in and live it.

As I've said, communicating your intentional culture to your employees goes well beyond stated messages. What employee programs do you have that reinforce your culture? One of my clients decided that "learning" was one of her company's values, so she implemented quarterly programs open to all employees to learn and grow. The company also had a very generous plan for ongoing education to reward employees who took it upon themselves to enhance their skills. Like this CEO, develop opportunities within your company to allow employees to use, communicate, and "live" your culture every day.

Now back to the lobby. Please, please, make what people first see when they enter your building (or office or store or website) consistent with your culture. Remember your first date? Didn't you want to make a good impression? You might think about this in terms of customers, but it matters for your employees too. Make sure everything you communicate both visually and verbally is aligned with your culture. Daily reinforcement contributes to employees feeling satisfied with their jobs—more so than money.

Communicating Your Intentional Culture to Your Customers

Though more and more initial contact occurs online, often the first human interaction you have with your customers is through the people who answer your phones. It's the rare business that never has phone contact with customers, so pay attention to this aspect of your company. One of the companies I work with changed their receptionist's title to "Director of First Impressions." (We'll talk more about titles in Chapter Four, so don't run out and change everyone's title before you read at least that far.) Not only did that change make the receptionist feel valued, it let the customers know that they too were very important to the firm. When your employees feel important, they take their jobs more seriously and they are more likely to communicate the company's values to the outside world. So think about what your first impression is communicating. When you get trapped in the automated voicemail loop, how important do you feel to the company on the other end of the phone? I feel like they don't want to talk to me, but I'll bet nine times out of ten they have a mission and vision statement on the wall that says otherwise.

I'm guessing you didn't scrimp on your website. Does it really cost that much more to have a friendly voice answer the phone? Probably not when you do a full cost-analysis—the number of customers you keep happy will more than pay the cost of a friendly greeting when someone calls. Now, assuming you have a person to answer the phone and your three words are "hungry, humble, and smart," what would that person have to do to communicate that culture? My guess is: pick up the phone quickly (smart), know exactly what to say (smart), be gracious when customers are upset (humble), and try to get customers to the right person to have their needs met quickly (hungry). Make sure your phone is being answered by someone who represents your culture, or you'll be judged based on theirs.

One of my clients owns a special effects equipment manufacturing company. They are a group of very friendly, creative people. They answer the phone by saying, "Thank you for calling CITC, where cool stuff is show tough!" How can you not help but smile when you hear this? Answering the phone this way tells the caller that these people are fun and creative, and that they appreciate the call. In other words, the greeting clearly reflects the company's culture.

Your marketing materials should also reflect your culture. Most marketing people could take a company that was "hungry, humble, and smart" and weave that culture into any product line from its packaging to its advertising. (If they don't start with your culture, you really need a different marketing company.) What you wouldn't want to see is an ad campaign that was misaligned with the company culture. Most products and services are available from several companies, but most cultures are unique.

Knowing that your culture is your most significant opportunity to differentiate your company from your competitors, make sure yours shows in your marketing materials and most importantly on your website. If your website frustrates your customers and potential customers, inevitably they are going to wonder how your company is going to take care of their business. We've all had the experience of going to a website only to encounter the "under construction" or "down for maintenance" banner, or links and tabs that go nowhere. Or the site is so difficult to navigate you can't possibly find what you're looking for in one or two clicks. Or how about my personal favorite: when you can't find a phone number. That just screams, "Don't call me!" If you prefer that people contact you via email (which is fine), make sure someone responds within twenty-four hours. If you don't, it says volumes about what your culture is and how you'll treat that customer in the future, if you get the chance.

Everyone at your firm (your sales people, account managers, service people, etc.) should "touch" the customer in a way that is consistent with your culture. If you hire for culture, you won't have difficulty training this. If you do not, you'll have to make some changes. Every customer interaction is a reflection of your company and you. Make sure every interaction demonstrates the correct image of your company.

Reinforcing Your Intentional Culture

Once you've identified your culture (hopefully with three words that are easy to communicate), you need to reinforce it on a regular basis. You can use your three words to go back and fine tune the final version of your mission, vision, and values statements. Just make sure that the values expressed in those statements are "lived" and felt every day in your company. One person moving against the culture of your organization will cause problems, and, if they are allowed to continue to do so, your aligned people will leave because the organization is not living its intentional culture.

So, what employee rewards programs do you have to honor those who live your culture in their work? For sales, it's relatively easy: if they sell more, their commission or bonus pay should reflect that. For internal employees, rewards (such as employee of the month or other recognition awards) should reflect very specific examples of culture success. And, if you're building a team-based culture, recognition should be based on the performance of the whole team, not just an individual.

All of your processes and systems need to stay in alignment with your culture. If your culture exists to treat employees and customers in a humble, smart, and hungry way, for instance, do your processes reflect this? Are there things you are doing that prevent systems from conforming to your culture? Examine how things run in your organization and listen to what your employees and customers have to tell you. If you hear that something is out of alignment from more than one person, chances are they're right. In a "smart" culture, you would encourage them to also have a solution, rather than waiting for you or a manager to fix it for them. Do your employees feel enabled to make something right for a customer? Is that in alignment with what you say your values and culture are?

Think of your company's intentional culture as a highway that has just been paved: The road signs are clear. There is no traffic congestion. Everyone knows which side of the road to drive on. All drivers know which direction they're headed and how to recognize when they get where they're going. Unintentional culture is more like driving on a dirt road, with no signs, and in the wrong kind of vehicle. What are the odds these drivers know where they're going and can actually get there? Is your organization's culture the paved road or the dirt road? Create the road you want or it will be created for you.

Intentional Culture Checklist

- ❒ Describe your Intentional Culture in three words.
- ❒ List at least three ways you'll communicate this to your employees.
- ❒ List at least three ways you'll communicate this to your customers.
- ❒ List the ongoing programs you have to reinforce the culture you've created. Do any of these need to be retooled or retired?
- ❒ Brainstorm several new ways to reinforce your culture.

Recommended Reading

The Art of the Start: The Time-Tested, Battle-Hardened Guide for Anyone Starting Anything, Guy Kawasaki, Portfolio Hardcover, 2004.

The Five Dysfunctions of a Team: A Leadership Fable, Patrick Lencioni, Jossey-Bass, 2002.

The Four Obsessions of the Extraordinary Executive: A Leadership Fable, Patrick Lencioni, Jossey-Bass, 2000.

Puzzle Piece Three
The CEO's Role

Being a CEO is first, middle, and last about leadership. Leadership is not primarily about control or power (although you'll have both, and you'll have to make the best decisions you can about how to use each at different times). True leadership is the ability to inspire others to rally around your culture and mission, and work toward a vision with you. Equally importantly, leadership is not about the leader: it's about recognizing that, if being a CEO were a one-person job, employees wouldn't be necessary.

Anyone can tell someone what to do, but not everyone can motivate follow through. If you're a parent, you've given orders with varying degrees of success. You've probably learned that your leadership isn't determined by the words coming out of your mouth, it's determined by your child's willingness to act positively on those words. The point at which your children start questioning your authority is where leadership starts. Why should they do what you say? What's in it for them? What does it look like if they do? Your ability to address those questions in a way that motivates positive action constitutes your leadership. What's more, if you've raised more than one child, you also know that they're each unique:

how each one responds to your leadership style will depend on who *they* are and what kind of leader *you* are.

The same is true with your employees. I've heard it said that, if it weren't for employees, running a business would be easy. But, if it weren't for employees, you wouldn't have a business at all, so thinking about how to be the best leader you can be makes a lot of practical sense. While you might be lucky and have a perfect employee, most of your employees are going to be ordinary people, and being a good leader means getting extraordinary results out of ordinary people on a regular basis. Good leaders do this by tapping into the deepest human need to be valued, and, in doing so, they draw out potential to fulfill a purpose, a goal, or a vision. These are the CEOs who understand that getting results comes as much or more from listening and responding: they are *not* about ego, they are about winning through and with others.

Let's imagine a portrait of a good leader to examine this in more depth. The CEO of a large medical practice constantly worked to grow as a leader, always wondering if he was doing things right. Eventually he came to realize that getting the best results is not about always *doing things right*. In fact, your people need to see you fail occasionally to know you're like them: human. When your people identify with you on a human level, they're more likely to trust you and be honest with you. And when you're honest with them, you can take the ego out of failure and use those moments as learning experiences for everyone. So good leadership is more about *doing the right things*. This CEO listens when people need him, he inspires, he promotes, he facilitates the direction of the company. He knows what he doesn't do well and hires others to do those things. He is truly viewed by the employees and the other doctors as a great leader, but he would never tell you that because he knows that his success is built on the success of the people he manages.

Leaders are people who motivate through action, thought, and word whenever each is called for. They are congruent in all three, and they live their values. People are drawn to people who do what they say they're going to do, even if it's unpopular. Politicians get low marks on the integrity and leadership scale because they often say what they think we want to hear and then say or do something else. So, if you want part of your culture to be to "have fun," what are *you* doing to have fun? If you say you value family, how much time do *you* spend with yours? Employees are looking to see if your behavior and the stated values of the organization match, and you usually have only one shot at getting this right. If you want your employees to use their vacation time because it's important to get rest, but then you cancel any vacation they haven't used at the end of the year, what message are you sending? How much vacation do you take yourself? Have you noticed that we all can't help but watch when a politician is taken down for being caught in a lie? Well, your employees are watching you just as closely.

Learning from Your Past Leadership Roles

Think about the times you've held leadership roles in your life. (You may have been class president, a scout leader, a team leader in sports.) What were you doing? What team did you put together? Think through your past leadership experiences and analyze how well you did. Did you like it? If you were uncomfortable the first time you were a leader, did you go back for seconds anyway? Did each subsequent leadership role get easier?

Really take a hard look at those experiences and scrutinize what you did well and what you would do differently. I used to be pretty hard on people, expecting everyone to move at my speed (fast!), which made the people around me, including myself, dizzy and often crazy. I realized that saying to people, consciously or unconsciously, "do what I do and don't ask questions" was not a great leadership strategy because it was all about me. Match people at their pace and lead them to yours.

Identifying Your Core Strengths or Talents

You cannot lead others unless you know what you do well and what you don't do well. In *Now, Discover Your Strengths*, Marcus Buckingham discusses thirty-five core strengths that exist across the spectrum of people. Out of those, five will resonate as major strengths in each of us. Buckingham's premise is that we can't improve on weaknesses, we can only enhance our strengths. Over time and with work, each of our core strengths can be cultivated into what Buckingham calls talents. I've employed this assumption with almost all the people I work with, and it has proven to be quite accurate.

So look at yourself: What are your core strengths? Are any of them talents yet? My guess is, if you're reading a book about being a CEO, you have several strengths that have become talents. Some of the CEOs I work with are phenomenal at understanding the numbers, some are great with people, some are inventors and thinkers, some are operational aces, some are strategic thinkers, some are execution wizards, and some are terrific at sales. Some have more than one major strength, but the ones who are great leaders know where they excel and where they do not. They don't pretend to be good in all areas, and they're quick to identify their own missing strengths in others.

What Talent Do You Need on Your Team?

There is a big difference between being the conductor and being first violin in the orchestra. One is about accomplishing a group goal and one is about accomplishing a personal goal. The conductor of the orchestra is a leader; the first violin is the best at a specific skill. Being the leader is not about playing all the instruments; rather it's about assigning the parts and making sure they sound right together. It's about seeing the big picture and making the music happen.

Great leaders play to their strengths, and hire to balance their weaknesses for the overall good of the company. They recognize where they bring value to the company, and they work from within that area of capability while bringing in others who have the strengths and talents they lack. Just as importantly, they also mentor others who share their strengths so that, one day, one of those people can step up to the CEO role.

The first step you need to take in determining what your role will be and what roles you need to hire for is to determine what areas of skill your business needs to fulfill your vision. Depending on the nature of your business, you might need skills in some or all of the following areas:

- Finance
- Strategy
- Sales
- Marketing
- Engineering
- Operations
- IT

- HR
- Design

There are many more areas of strength, of course, but it's important first to identify which are yours and not pretend you can do it all. Once you've identified what *you* do well, you can identify or bring on others who can augment what you do best. In a small company, you will likely wear many hats to start with, but the sooner you can grow the talent around you, the better off your company will be. Keeping you in your area of strength while leading the organization will be enough of a challenge without having to wear *all* the hats. The most successful CEOs decide which of the many hats in the business they're going to wear, then they give the others away quickly and don't put them back on. The fewer hats you wear, the more successful you'll be. This is just delegating, right? But the key here is not just to hand out jobs. Hand them out intentionally. Figure out what you can do better than anyone else, and delegate the rest to people who can do it better than you. Then coach and manage those people so they excel.

In addition to the very practical reason that you really can't do it all, there are important psychological reasons to delegate wisely. Remember, being a great leader is about inspiring others. What kind of message does it send your employees when their boss does everything? Very simply, it tells them that they're incompetent or even untrustworthy, and that does *not* tap into their deepest human need to be valued. The CEOs who believe they can do everything better and faster than their employees will experience high turnover (and, quite frankly, they'll be lonely and tired). Why would anyone want to work for someone who always makes them feel inferior?

Here's another way to look at this: only do what only you can do. Wisely delegate the rest of it so you can focus on the company as a whole. The sooner you realize what it is only you can do, the sooner you can put together a great team to work with.

Delegating Wisely

Now that you've examined your own leadership role, I hope you're excited about delegating wisely. Later in this chapter, I'll talk in depth about how to structure and choose your executive team, but let's set some basic guidelines now so the system you put in place actually supports your role as leader. In a larger company (50 or more employees) you'll want to have three to five direct reports who take care of those areas of responsibility you've identified as being outside your most valuable skill set. Four or five reports is ideal. Too few reports will leave you still wearing too many hats. Too many won't leave you enough time to coach each of them while still providing strategic direction for the company. If your company is smaller (only a handful of employees), you'll need to wear more hats for a while. Prioritize those roles in terms of where your real value lies, and use that to dictate whom you bring in as you are ready to expand. Hire to delegate those roles you are weakest at first.

One CEO I worked with had fourteen direct reports. This was not her original intent, but the company grew faster than expected and the structure wasn't in place to implement deeper levels of management. Needless to say, everyone was unhappy and frazzled with the situation. We immediately identified the four roles needed to manage the company, and then worked to put those four people in place to report to the CEO. The company is now doing much better and employee satisfaction is at an all time high.

Creating a One Year Vision

The best way to avoid being taken by surprise with the makeup of your executive team is to plan ahead by creating a one-year vision. Your one-year vision will allow you to clarify what positions need to be filled and under what terms, while also thinking strategically about who to fill those with.

Businessman Pat Powers once said, "We hire people for what they can do and fire them for who they are." I love this comment because it's so painfully true. We so often look at a person's skills and assume that's who they are. And then, time after time, we're surprised when the real person shows up. But, if you've read the preceding chapters, you'll know why hiring for skills alone doesn't work. I recommend that, before you hire your key people, you take a step back and examine what you really need to accomplish in the next year. Or, if your team is already in place, take a second look at them based on what needs to be accomplished, and, conversely, what has not been accomplished that you had hoped would be. Taking a moment to reflect on your goals will help you be smarter about putting together your executive team.

If you're in start-up mode, there are a lot of things that need to happen in short order, and, more often than not, cash will be a critical factor. Nonetheless, before you dive into that stack of resumes, take some time to review your Intentional Purpose in order to gain a real understanding of the skill sets and key positions your company needs in order to succeed over the next year. We'll talk about how to choose people who fit your culture in Chapter Four, but first you need to clarify the positions you need to fill. Let's start by setting out some basic guidelines.

First, don't get caught in the trap of thinking that the structure you're implementing now is permanent. Some positions are strictly start-up, temporary, or contract. For example, perhaps you need a good finance person for year one to get the business on a solid footing, but having someone full-time in that position might be overkill on an ongoing basis. A contract CFO might fit the bill for now, and you can always readjust expectations for the position as your business develops. If Research and Development are a top priority, don't hesitate to get the best you can for the money right from the start because time to market is critical. If immediate sales are necessary, then hire a hunter and let that person loose! The point is to prioritize your needs, define the positions, and hire accordingly.

If your team is already in place, take a hard look at what has and has not been accomplished. What is your vision for the next couple of years? What are the strengths and weaknesses of your team in light of that vision? If you had to do it all over again, would you hire the same people with the same skills? Resets are a continuous part of running a successful business, but we're often reluctant to do so with people. Don't be, or you'll have trouble meeting your growth goals. Consider yourself in start-up mode. Go through the thought process outlined in the paragraph above and then apply it to your current executive team. What do you see when you look through a reset lens? You might be surprised, both positively and negatively. Now, based on what you see, make the changes necessary to achieve the vision of your organization.

What Key Reports Do You Need to Implement Your Vision?

From of the following list you should be able to identify three to five positions you'll need to create right away or sometime in the first year.

These will ideally become your executive management team:

- Chief Financial Officer (CFO)
- Chief Information Officer (CIO)
- Chief Innovation Officer (CIO)
- Chief Investment Officer (CIO)
- Chief Operating Officer (COO)
- Chief Technical Officer (CTO)
- Chief Administration Officer (CAO, most often in healthcare)
- Chief Marketing Officer (CMO)
- Chief Learning Officer (CLO)
- Chief Legal Officer (CLO)
- Chief Science Officer (CSO)
- Chief Human Resource Officer (CHRO)
- President (of divisions or company)
- Executive Vice President (EVP)
- Vice Presidents (of divisions or company)
- Human Resources Director
- Marketing Director
- Sales Director
- Research & Development Director
- Engineering Director
- Project Manager
- Recruiting Director
- Controller

In identifying key positions, focus on the key areas of your company. Look back at the skills list. Which three focus areas are key to achieving your company's vision? For example, a typical manufacturing company might have someone in charge of Operations or Production; someone in charge of HR and Administration; someone in charge of Sales; someone in charge of Finance; and possibly someone in charge of Engineering. A creative services company might have someone in charge of Creative Development or Marketing; someone in charge of Administration or Operations; and possibly people in charge of different product categories.

Regardless of the title, make sure the positions as you are defining them are aligned with your company's needs and goals. Of course, when a company is small, everyone will wear multiple hats to accomplish overall goals, while continuing to *lead* in their respective area of expertise. Just make sure all essential leadership bases are covered and you don't have a gap in coverage. Think of this like an insurance adjuster would: what are the risks and how should they be mitigated? If you are going through a reset, do a S.W.O.T. analysis of the organizational chart. What changes do you need to make? Don't be afraid to cut or move people around based on the company's needs and the skills of the individuals. Allowing yourself to do this could mean the difference between your company's success and failure. And you might find that, even with some initial stress, everyone is happier in the long run when their roles are aligned with the company's goals. (See the end of this chapter for more information about how to do a S.W.O.T. analysis and letting employees go.)

Titles and Entitlement

Be very careful with titles. Once given, it's almost impossible to take a title away without significant negative consequences. Not to mention the precedent it sets for the organization. When creating positions always go back to the key questions: What is your company's vision? What are your company's values? Create positions wisely and fill them intentionally. When you do these two things, you'll have to fill them less frequently.

If you only have twenty-five people in your company, you probably don't need C-level executives yet. If you want to give some of your people those titles because they've done a good job and you want to make them feel important, stop and think through some of the potential negative consequences first. There's lots of information out there about "comparable" positions, and I promise you people will interpret the information they find to their own benefit. One of my clients gave the title "bookkeeper" to an entry-level administrative position. After three months, the employee wanted a huge raise because a quick internet search showed she was being underpaid for someone with that title. Additionally, C-level executives in a fifty-person company are going to compare themselves to C-level executives of a five hundred-person company and expect comparable pay, even though the responsibilities are almost always different.

Have you ever tried to take a title away from someone? Reneging on a title is just like hanging a sign on that person that says, "I didn't make it." It's a rare occurrence when someone could actually go back to doing a previous position after getting a promotion or title change. Keep your positions and titles aligned with the Intentional Purpose of the company. If an actual promotion isn't really warranted, resist the urge to give a new title as a reward. Find another way to reward a good employee.

Creating Your Executive Team

The process you go through to create your Executive Team will be emulated by your direct reports to create theirs. Make sure that process is worthy of repeating. Be a mentor. If you've made mistakes, share them. If you've done something that worked well, share that. You never win by withholding information from your team. Some CEOs do this to make themselves feel smarter or to "test" their teams. Both strategies make you look weak and ineffective in the end. One CEO I worked with had a management meeting and told his six key reports to prepare a PowerPoint presentation about what was happening in their departments. He gave them three days to prepare. Three of them, however, had never prepared their own PowerPoint presentations; they had only used ones prepared for them. When it came time to present, the CEO went first and gave an elaborate display. He then asked each of his people to present in succession and was visibly agitated when the rest were not, to his mind, as good as his.

How motivating do you think this experience was to people who were trying to learn something new? Instead of an educational experience, it turned into humiliation for two of them. I'm certain this was not the CEO's intent. But remember, the outcome will often "rewrite" the intent, and that is the story that will be told and retold. Always state your intention and make sure your actions follow from that. Heck, everything I know I got from other people or by doing the opposite of what I should have done. Why make your team reinvent the wheel when you probably didn't do that yourself? Besides, putting your team through this kind of pointless exercise only distracts and detracts from the work they should be doing for the company.

While you need to be a mentor to develop your key people, don't settle for someone who *might* be good in *any* position. If a person's past work doesn't demonstrate the specific behavior you're looking for, the likelihood is small that you will see it in the future. Remember Marcus Buckingham's premise that you can't work on weaknesses, only strengths. Another way to look at this is that past performance predicts future behavior. No matter how great a leader you think you are, you can't make a duck bark.

Focus on the behaviors you know are required by the position and that are nonnegotiable. The only way to predict if someone meets these is by asking behavior-based interview questions grounded in the Job Description you've created (see Chapter Four for more details on behavior-based interviewing). Remember, an interview is one of the best performances your potential employee will ever give you. Be honest with yourself: if you are terrible at interviewing, get someone to help you. One bad hire will cost you three times the annual salary you are advertising for a position.

And no, you can't hire someone without having a job description because they won't know how their performance will be measured, and thus can't accurately tell you whether they can do the job or not. Writing a job description is a prerequisite to interviewing for any position, but particularly for your Executive Team. So think about your goals and the positions you need to fulfill those, and then get to work writing your job descriptions. See Chapter Four for a more in-depth discussion of job descriptions, but very briefly a simple job description should contain the following:

- Job duties and responsibilities
- *Required* skills and characteristics
- *Desired* skills and characteristics

Once you've defined your team, spend some time thinking about what the team needs to accomplish in the first year. Set a strategy, milestones, and goals, and communicate those clearly to everyone.

Grow Your People and Your Company

When I'm asked what I think the CEO's job is, I say it's only two things:

1. Grow your People
2. Grow your Company

And then I ask the CEO, "Whose job are you doing right now?" Every CEO I have asked this question of has smiled sheepishly and said, "Well, but ...". They were all doing someone else's job. Good CEOs don't make excuses for why something isn't going right, they *make* it right. If you had all the money, time, and talent in the world your business would succeed in spite of you, but unfortunately none of these resources are unlimited. The truly great CEOs know how to lead in the absence of one or all of those three resources because they focus on growing their people and growing their companies.

People

So, what *are* you doing to grow your people? Do they even know you're interested in their development? If not, you had better communicate that vision to them or they'll make one up about how you don't care. If you have three or four direct reports, you can spend time with each of them finding out what their personal goals are for their careers, and looking for ways to fit that into your company. This will also teach them how to develop those who report to them. If your direct reports feel cared for and respected, they will in turn treat their own teams with care and respect.

If, on the other hand, you are coaching and your direct reports are not, open a conversation and evaluate whether or not they belong in that managerial role. So often in organizations I find great people who are simply in the wrong job or the wrong company at the wrong time. Grow them, move them into another position in your business, or help them transition out to another company.

Growing your people means mentoring, but it also means being honest about their strengths *and* weaknesses. A software company I worked with had a VP who had moved up through the ranks and was essentially leading the company. The CEO felt comfortable with the VP in that role because he had "earned" it through years of dedication to the company. Unfortunately, the VP's one weakness was accountability: he never delivered a project on time. Remember that weaknesses are almost never fixable, and, in this case, that weakness trumped his dedication because it negatively impacted everyone who worked with him as well as the company as a whole. By the time the CEO saw past his personal loyalty and made a change, the company had almost folded. No one should earn a position simply through loyalty or longevity: they have to have the corresponding skills (or strengths that can be mentored into skills) to be successful in the position. Your job in growing your people is to reward their strengths, while also being candid about their weaknesses.

Company

Your role in growing your company is to be the thought leader. What strategic opportunities are out there to capitalize on? What new products or services can you bring to market? How can you do something different and create your company around it? Think about Starbucks. Who knew we would all be paying four dollars for a cup of coffee and not resent that? We were willing to do that because Starbucks created an atmosphere around coffee that hadn't existed before, and that was what we paid for. Does Howard Schultz live and breathe his company's culture? And is he all about growing his people and his company? Absolutely! And Starbucks employees know it. How else could they be so friendly and happy when you order your double mocha Frappuccino, light, no whip latte?

See, it's really that simple. Use your CEO Job Description to keep yourself on track as a great leader:

- Only do what only you can do
- Grow your people
- Grow your company

Put a Post-It note on your computer monitor as a reminder to ask yourself: "Whose job am I doing right now?" If you have to, put it on a t-shirt, or a cap, or a mug. Go for it. This job is tough enough without something to remind us to smile every now and then. But the bottom line is, if you're doing too many other jobs for very long, no one will be doing yours and your company will fail.

Additional Resources

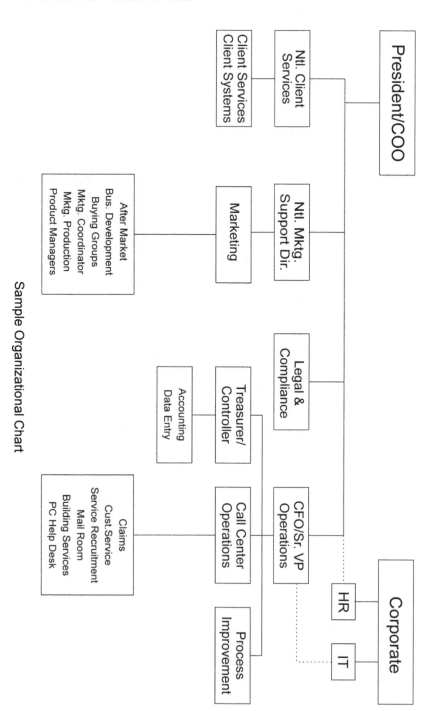

Sample Organizational Chart

How to Do a S.W.O.T. Analysis

As its name suggests a S.W.O.T. analysis is a tool for examining the positives and negatives within your business as well as in the outside environment. Strengths and Weaknesses are often defined as identifying issues *internal* to the businesses, while Opportunities and Threats identify issues *external* to the business. It can be helpful to frame the exercise this way, though clearly that will be specified a little differently if you are doing a S.W.O.T. analysis on something like your organizational chart as opposed to your market position. You can hire an outside professional to perform a S.W.O.T. analysis, but you can also use S.W.O.T. with your management team to do a quick check in of any aspect of your business, from strategic planning to a single project. Think of the S.W.O.T. format as a simple way to direct a conversation that will reveal the most urgent problems to be solved and actions to be taken.

If you are going to do a S.W.O.T. analysis as a group exercise or with input from key people, start by identifying the relevant individuals. They might be your executive team, or your managers, or it might be the people who lead in important areas whether they manage anyone or not. Prior to the meeting, ask them to bring their ideas about what currently is and isn't working for the particular issue or aspect of your business you are examining.

Once everyone is together, start by having a discussion about what *is* working (Strengths). Jot down all those statements as they are made. Emphasize that there are no right or wrong answers; all opinions are valid. Don't edit at this point or you'll shut down the conversation. Next list everything that isn't working (Weaknesses). Then do the same for Opportunities and Threats. Sometimes people have trouble distinguishing between a Weakness and a Threat. This is where the internal (Weakness) vs. external (Threat) distinction can be particularly helpful.

Once your chart is complete, identify the most important items to take action on. As you examine the chart, you might find that there are redundancies. Some items might even appear in different categories. But that's why it's really important not to edit too early in the process. Items that appear multiple times or in different places on the chart are likely to be important and deserve further discussion. Places where you see similarities or common themes should be your highest priorities for action.

Letting an Employee Go

Firing someone is never easy, but it can be done in a way that protects both your company and the dignity of the employee. The first step is to make sure you have tried to help the employee remedy the situation. If the issue is skills based, have you given them the appropriate feedback and training or made sure they know where to get it? Have you made it clear that following through on that is a job requirement? If it's become apparent the person truly lacks the skills for their current position, is there any other position they could be successful in and are qualified for? If the answer to all of the above questions is no, then you can proceed to the three step termination process described in Chapter Four.

If the problem is behavior based, make sure you've talked specifically about the behavior you are looking for, the behavior you cannot tolerate, and what the outcome will be if it does not change. Proceed with the three-step process, and be sure to let the employee know that there is not a deadline by which to rectify the intolerable behavior. The change needs to occur immediately and be ongoing.

Once you've made the decision to terminate someone, be sure to check with your HR professional, outside resource, or employment attorney so that you can be sure to adhere to the proper procedures and applicable law for this situation. Then call the person into your office and be sure to have another person present. It's always good to have a witness to what was said, for safety sake. Let the employee know that you are doing one of two things: 1.) eliminating the position; or 2.) letting them go for cause as described in the written warnings. Ask the person if they have any questions, but do not go into long explanations. Keep your discussion brief and focused on the specific behavioral shortfall described in the written warning. Let the person know what the terms are (for example if they will receive a severance package as described in your employee handbook) and give them their final paycheck. Mutually agree to a time at a later date for the person to return for their personal items (it is usually embarrassing for them to return to their office or cubicle immediately after being terminated), and then be prepared to escort them out.

None of this is easy for anyone, not least the person being fired. Always remember that you are dealing with a person. People handle upset differently, so be as calm and kind as you can be. Don't be mean or rude. But also never justify your position or go into long explanations. If you've followed the three-step procedure, once you get to step three, the decision has been made, period.

CEO Checklist

☐ Describe three times you've been in a leadership role.

☐ Identify what you did well or what worked for you in each role.

☐ Identify what didn't work well and what you would do differently.

☐ Identify your core strengths (if you're having trouble with this, ask a colleague, friend, or your partner what they think).

☐ Put a star next to the core strength that is most important for your company.

☐ Describe your one-year vision. (Another way to think about this is, what needs to happen in the next year?)

☐ List the skills you need on your team.

☐ Looking at those skills, list the positions you'll need on your team in order to fulfill your one-year vision (write the title and whether it's a long- or short-term position)?

☐ Name the people already in your company who have those skills and fit your culture for each of these positions. (If that person doesn't already work for your company, make a note to fill the position and be sure to read Chapter Four on hiring.)

☐ List the things you're doing to grow your people.

☐ List the things you're doing to grow your company.

Recommended Reading

The Dream Manager, Matthew Kelly, Hyperion, 2007.

First, Break all the Rules: What the World's Greatest Managers Do Differently, Marcus Buckingham, Simon & Schuster, 1999.

The Five Temptations of a CEO, Patrick Lencioni, Jossey-Bass, 1998.

Good to Great: Why Some Companies Make the Leap ... and Others Don't, Jim Collins, HarperBusiness, 2001.

Leadership and Self-Deception: Getting Out of the Box, The Arbinger Institute, BerrettKoehler Publishers, 2010.

Play to Win!: Choosing Growth Over Fear in Work and Life, Larry Wilson, Hersch Wilson, and Ken Blanchard, Bard Press, 2004.

Primal Leadership: Learning to Lead with Emotional Intelligence, Daniel Goleman, Harvard Business Review Press, 2004.

What Got You Here Won't Get You There: How Successful People Become Even More Successful, Marshall Goldsmith and Mark Reiter, Hyperion, 2007.

Puzzle Piece Four
Hiring

A company's most valuable asset is usually its people. Nonetheless, while businesses put a lot of resources into research for product development, they frequently leave the selection and training of human "assets" to untrained professionals, to guesswork, or to the belief that you can teach anyone to do something just because you like them. These assumptions are just as costly for a company as going to market with a product that won't sell.

There is so much information available about hiring that it can be a daunting task to sort through it all and decide what will work best for your company and your values. The method I see most often at entrepreneurial companies is improvisational: "Let's give it a try and see if it works." Unfortunately, in most cases, hiring this way does not. And when your hiring process doesn't work, it's a costly failure. Finding and interviewing candidates for a position should be a *slow* process, like dating before you get married. You want to date for as long as it takes before you commit because, as anyone who's been through one knows, divorce is usually messy, emotional, time consuming, and expensive. Firing someone often is too. So let's walk through how to develop an intentional process for hiring and retaining the best candidates for your company.

Job Description and Salary Range

To continue with the dating analogy, think of this step as a profile on a dating site. Without a clear job description, how will you know when you find the right candidate? You have to be clear about the desired profile or anyone you interview can *seem* like the right fit. As I mentioned in Chapter Three, I'm a big believer in a simple job description that includes:

- Job duties and responsibilities
- *Required* skills and characteristics
- *Desired* skills and characteristics

If you have a one or two page description incorporating these three items, you have a great start to your *intentional* hiring process. Your job description will allow you to identify the behaviors that will form the basis of your behavior-based interview questions, and that will reveal whether or not a candidate will be able to perform the job to your specifications. More detailed job descriptions are fine, just be sure to identify the *key* characteristics and skills required for a successful hire. Most importantly, don't forget to declare your mission and values. If you hire for a values match, the rest gets a lot easier.

I recommend creating a salary range for every position in your company. By doing this before hiring, you set salary expectations early and you avoid the problem of employees expecting a raise every year just for sticking around. Another reason to set salary ranges in advance is that it helps establish a culture that pays for performance not longevity. Furthermore, when you have established a salary range based on research of comparable positions, it becomes much easier to say "no" when an employee at the top of the pay range asks for a raise because you've already established the fair ceiling for the position. Ambitious employees who want to earn a salary beyond the range for that position can request more training, take on added responsibility, or go to school on their own. Or, if one of your organizational values is learning, perhaps you can establish a program that reinforces additional training or education to help those talented or high-potential employees stay engaged or advance into new positions.

In setting salary ranges, it's important to conduct some outside research on pay ranges for your industry and for each job. You want to be fair and aware of what market conditions are in your region and industry so you can attract and retain top talent. Getting a "bargain" on an employee is likely to backfire on you in the future when that person finds out what their marketable skills are worth to the industry. They will want more money or they will leave, and neither of these is a conversation you want to have frequently. Fortunately there are multiple resources for salary surveys. One of the most popular of these is www.salary.com, but you can also easily do research with geographic- or industry-based parameters.

Your employees have probably already done their own research and found out what salary ranges are for their positions. If anything, they will put themselves in a higher classification than you would. Remember the "bookkeeper" I talked about in Chapter Three? The company hired young, unskilled help for accounting clerical positions and paid them twelve to fourteen dollars an hour. When they renamed that position "bookkeeper," the employee did her research on what a bookkeeper typically makes and came back, survey in hand, demanding twenty dollars per hour, although her skills and experience hadn't changed. Had the company had an accurate job description, title, and salary range set in advance, this awkward situation could have been avoided altogether.

Determine Your Hiring Process

When your company's most important asset is the people who represent you and do the work, it's critical to have an established process for recruiting and hiring. Hiring is, in fact, the most important process in your business. In developing your hiring process you will need to determine the following:

- Whether you will be recruiting internally (using your own people) or externally (using a recruiter).
- What types of assessment tools (personality assessments and skills tests) you'll be using, and at what point in the process.
- What other additional screening you need to do.
- How you will verify work histories.
- How you will rank candidates.
- How you will conduct interviews, and what you will ask.

Let's look at each of these points in more depth.

Recruiting

Recruiting means how your future employees find you, or how you find them. You can choose to have this done internally by your HR department or you can hire an outside firm to recruit for you. If you are too small to have an HR department, this task will fall to whomever you have designated as the hiring manager for the position (it might even be you).

Internal Recruiting: Recruiting internally should involve all your company's employees. If they are happy, they will tell others, creating a pipeline of ready, willing, and able employees. This is sometimes easier for the less skilled positions, but nevertheless works at all levels. One company I know of provides business cards to all employees to hand out to anyone they see doing an outstanding job. The card says "You are a Star, and this card entitles you to an interview at XYZ Company." This provides a great opportunity for all your employees to be constant recruiters for you. An architectural firm I work with offers a one-week cruise to any employee who recruits an architect that is successfully hired and stays on after six months. Some companies pay finder's fees to employees who bring in someone who is ultimately hired. I used to pay a finder's fee of $500 upon hiring the new employee, $500 at six months, and $500 at a year. This gave some incentive for the referral employee to help keep the new employee happy. I've also seen cases where the new employee was also given the fee, thus creating a bond between the two employees. Don't be afraid to use nonmonetary incentives as well. For instance, time off is always a good motivator.

Job listings should always be posted on the company website in addition to other venues. While this might seem obvious, I'm amazed by how often this easy recruiting tool is overlooked. Create a jobs section with a listing of all the jobs available, why someone would want to work for your company, and a statement about your values. Highlight the three required behaviors for that job and tie them to your values. Make sure your website jobs listings and ads are always up to date.

External Recruiting: I've worked with some great recruiters and some really bad recruiters. Some agencies don't truly recruit; they just place ads for you, wait until someone answers, and then prepare the candidate to interview with you. By definition a "recruiter" should go out and seek candidates for your positions, usually contacting people who are already employed. You will typically pay 7–100% of the position's annual salary as a "fee" for this hire with a guarantee of 30–180 days retention depending on the level of the position. Some agencies will work on a fixed-fee basis with the understanding that you will not use other recruiters (this is called a "sole and exclusive contract").

Because you'll be making a significant investment not only in your future employee, but also in the process of finding that person, choose your recruiting partner carefully. Speak to other clients who have had successful placements and find out what that recruiter's track record is for successful hires. You might need to hire a recruiter who works by specialty (for example accounting, executive placements, engineering, etc.). Choose a recruiter who will take the time to get to know your company: your culture, the position, the responsibilities, and what it will take for a hire to be successful. And always read the contract carefully to determine your obligations if you find a candidate on your own.

Resume Ranking and Prescreening Candidates

Once you have a stack of resumes, you need to develop a way to rank them. The larger firms have software that sorts by words or word groups, but most of us don't have that luxury. One way to rank resumes is to take the behavioral traits and industry experience you are looking for and assign points to each. For example, you might rank the attributes and assign five points for the most important down to one point for the least important. Or, if all attributes are equally important, give each one two points for a maximum point total of two times the total number of traits you are looking for. Whichever method you choose, determine in advance the minimum total points a resume must score for moving forward in the process. The key to success with a point system is not to deviate from whatever procedure you set up. Always apply the point system the same way to each resume. Now scan your stack of resumes for these traits and simply give each a score. Any candidates falling below the minimum score are eliminated from the process at this point.

After all your resumes have been ranked as described above, someone will need to do initial phone screening to determine if you want to spend time on in-person interviews. If you have an HR department, this will be one of their tasks. If you're using a recruiter, they should do this for you. If the task falls on you or one of your managers, develop about three questions based on the job description that will give you a sense of the person on the phone. (Obviously if the phone is a big part of the job and they have a terrible phone manner, you won't invite them in for an interview.) Once you have several candidates who have passed the initial phone screen, you can begin the process of in-person interviewing as described below.

Now I know some of you will claim you dread the interview process because it's been unsuccessful in the past, or because you believe you're not good at it. Keep in mind, however, that poor hiring outcomes are often the result of no process or a process that wasn't followed correctly. So, stick to the process you've created and a positive outcome is likely to occur. And, as I've said before, if interviewing is not your area of expertise, assign it to one of your executive team members or outsource it.

Developing the Interview Process

Interview Team

The first step in the interview process is to create your interviewing team. This could be you and the direct manager, or you and two other managers (preferably the HR manager, if you have one) who will be coworkers of the position, or it could involve someone who would be a direct report to the new position. I recommend having at least three people on the team and probably no more than six, as that can be overkill.

Before you start the process, be sure to determine who will make the ultimate hiring decision, and who has veto authority if there is not total agreement. You don't want to have misunderstandings about how much say each person will have in the hiring process after you've already started. Define it up front. If it needs to be a unanimous vote, just be sure to spell it out before you start.

Finalizing The Process

Once you've decided on your hiring team and you've determined how the decision will be made, take some time to finalize the remainder of your process. Determine in advance how you'll conduct interviews and what questions you'll ask. This is also a good time to make decisions about other aspects of your evaluation process, including assessments and other screening tools and verification of work histories. Now you have everything in place to determine your actual interview strategy.

Interview Strategy

I once heard a hiring expert recommend a three by three interview strategy: three different interviews in three different places with three different people at three different times (of course for some less-skilled positions three interviews is too many, while for higher-level executive positions you might conduct more). This is a useful strategy because, let's face it, when someone is interviewing, they're on their best behavior. If you follow the three by three guideline, you'll have multiple opportunities to glean important information about candidate behaviors: for example, how they dress on three occasions, if they are late or on time, or how they behave at a restaurant (this might be a good indicator of manners). Conducting interviews in this way also shows that you are serious about finding the right person for the position. It demonstrates value to your prospective employee because you're clearly not willing to hire just anyone who walks in the door.

> **Locations:** I suggest the first interview be set up at the office, the second can be at a restaurant, and the third at a coffee shop or different location at the company. Across the three interviews, you are looking for consistency as well as behavior that is aligned with your company values and the position. If someone has horrible table manners, you would not want that person in a sales position. If a candidate arrives late because of traffic, this can be an indicator of a lack of planning skills. Everything about the interviews matters. Remember, you're evaluating behavior, and behavior is predictive of future performance.

> **Interviewers:** The key to having multiple people interview someone successfully is to have everyone ask the same questions. Plan to develop up to ten questions for each position you are interviewing for. Each interviewer will ask the same questions and then, once all the interviews are complete, they'll compare the answers. You're looking for consistency in the way the interviewee answers no matter who the interviewer is and no matter what the location.

It's important to remember that the interviewing team should not get together until all the interviews have taken place. You don't want to prejudice an interviewer before they've had the opportunity to conduct the interview.

Times: Interviewing at various times of the day allows you to see if your interviewees are as sharp at eight o'clock in the morning as they are at three o'clock in the afternoon.

Developing Interview Questions

Identifying Specific Behavioral Traits: Before you start developing your interview questions, go back to your job description and identify three or four behavioral traits that you'll be interviewing for. You're not really looking for personality characteristics; you're looking for specific behavioral traits that are required for the job. Some examples might be:

- Outside Sales—Hunter, independent, competitive
- Controller—Detailed, patient, confidential
- Engineer—Creative, flexible, process-oriented
- Customer Service—Adaptable, results-oriented, friendly
- Service Technician—Timely, creative, technical

You can see how the list for any given position could be quite long. If you come up with five or six based on your job description, stick to the top three or four to develop into questions, but be looking for examples of the others.

Behavior-Based Questions: This is really the key to good interviewing, and consequently good hiring. Almost everyone has participated in an interview where the interviewer said: "Tell me about your good traits?" Or my favorite: "Tell me what you need to improve?" While these are interesting to know, they are most often not a real predictor of the interviewee's behavior, and in some cases the answers will be totally made up. For one thing, most people are very self-*un*aware: they simply won't have a clue how to answer and will come up with something just to answer the question. Moreover, women will tend to tell you they are terrible at several things they are actually good at, while men will tell you they are great at everything. I know this sounds horribly sexist, but I also know I have experienced it in hiring, and I'm sure you have as well. So, the bottom line is, while they are typical interview queries, those types of questions don't tell you what you want to know.

Open-ended, behavior-based questions are the very best way to elicit the kinds of answers that will give you real information about how a candidate is likely to perform within your company and in the position you're hiring for. Once you've established which behavioral traits are key to success in this position, you can develop questions around those specific traits. Let's say you're looking for a sales person who really goes out there and creates new business (as opposed to an account manager who takes care of existing accounts), your first question might be: "Tell me about a time when you had to develop a new account." Hopefully the candidate will be able to tell you about one, and then you can ask follow up questions based on what you heard. If a candidate cannot tell you about a specific incidence, then it didn't happen. Or, if the candidate makes up an answer, and you're doing three different interviews with the same questions, the story is unlikely to be the same all three times and you'll know that the candidate is not being truthful.

I recommend coming up with ten questions because ten is enough to elicit information about all the behaviors you're looking for, but it's not so many that you'll totally drain the person you're interviewing. And by asking the same ten questions in each of the interviews, when your team gets together to debrief, you are really comparing apples to apples.

See the end of this chapter for a list of behavior-based interview questions.

Resume Review: In addition to asking behavior-based questions, another helpful way to find out about a candidate's behaviors is to have the person walk you through their resume from oldest position to most recent. Listen for their reasons for transitioning from one position to another, as well as for what they say and don't say about each company where they worked. Take notes, but save your follow-up questions for after you've asked the scripted behavior-based questions. This exercise can give you a sense of patterns in their work history, while providing you with specific points to follow up on if there is a particular job on their resume you wanted to know more about.

Other Questions: Another important way to match people to your culture is to devise interview questions around the values you identified in Chapter One as essential to your company (remember from Chapter Two that Culture = Lived Values). If one of those values happens to be "fun," have your candidate describe what a fun workplace looks like to them. When have they had fun on the job? Remember you want them to tell you their version, not repeat back what you have told them is yours.

The last question I always ask in an interview is: "If I were to offer you the job today, would you take it?" This is a great way to assess whether or not the candidate is really interested in moving forward. You don't want to waste your time keeping this person in the candidate pool if the answer isn't an honest and excited "Yes!" to the possibility of moving forward with your company. It's no fun to call someone you think is terrific to make an offer, only to have that person tell you they don't actually want the job. When this happens you have to move to your second choice, and, somehow, candidates always finds out they were not number one. That's not a great way to start a new job.

Evaluating Interviews

When you start interviewing, throw out the resume ranking because you're starting fresh with the in-person interview. At this point all of the interviewers will be working from the same ten behavior-based questions. Because each question examines a particular behavioral trait, you can give each good answer one point and no points for an answer that was weak or vague. This way, when you get together with the rest of the hiring team to compare interviews, you have a concrete starting point. This doesn't mean you'll hire the candidate with the highest score, it simply means you have a place to start the discussion.

A word of caution: all the work you do in the interview process is predicated on the assumption that you have vetted each candidate for the education and skills required by the position *prior* to interviewing. Why would you interview someone without a college degree if you stated that as a requirement of the job? And be very careful and explicit about what is really required. If a qualification is preferred but not required, say that in the job description. You don't want to get caught in a potential discrimination lawsuit because you decided to hire someone who has the skills but not the education you were looking for or vice versa.

Assessment Tools

In addition to strategic interviewing, you'll most likely want to use some kind of assessment tool to augment the interview process. Some tools, such as Personalysis, will only be appropriate for final candidates in key positions. Others, such as Behavior Styles, are short and inexpensive enough to be worth considering to test for candidate fit (StrengthsFinder is another short assessment that can be used for any position). Whichever assessment tools you choose, remember to be consistent in how you use them: decide ahead of time which tools you'll use and at what at point in the process, and apply those to every candidate for a position. Also be sure you explain to candidates what the tool is and how it's important to your company and the position. Your candidates will feel more positive and excited about the job they're interviewing for if they understand that you're trying to ensure a good fit and long-term success.

Tools for Matching People to Culture

As I've said, in hiring you're looking not only to match a person's specific skills to a job description, but, equally importantly, to match who they are as a person (their behaviors and character) to both the position and to your company as a whole. Most of the successful hiring I've been involved with has had some component of temperament or personality evaluation. There are a variety of assessments available for employers to choose from, and I'll discuss some of them in more detail below. Keep in mind that those designed to assess behavioral traits (also called temperament or personality) are better predictors of long-term fit and success within your company than those designed simply to assess skills, though both have their place in your hiring process.

One of the most popular personality assessments is the **Myers-Briggs**, which sorts individuals into one of sixteen different personality types based on preferences within four categories of experience. (You may be familiar with the four-letter personality types discerned by the Meyers-Briggs test.) This test has the advantage of being easy and inexpensive to administer, and it may give you some basic information on the type of person you're dealing with. But, unless you have some training in interpreting the Meyers-Briggs for professional settings, it can be hard to implement the results as a hiring methodology. For instance, unless you know for sure that a controller should be an "INTJ," knowing that your candidate is an "INTJ" doesn't help you understand how that personality type is going to behave in that position.

The **Personalysis Profile** is an expanded version of Myers-Briggs that not only measures personality type, but also makes predictions about how a person is likely to behave (think, feel, and interact) in particular situations. This type of profile can give you important information on how your prospective hires go about key functions such as goal setting and follow through, communicating, making decisions, working in teams, and accepting and giving guidance. I've found this type of profile exceptionally useful because it gives you concrete information about whether or not an individual is likely to succeed in the specific position you are interviewing for. More globally, these measures can tell you right away if a candidate is going to fit into your company's communication or leadership culture, as well as how you might need to adapt in order to ensure that person's success. On the flip side, the Personalysis company can generate an ideal candidate profile based on information you give them about the position and your company's culture. While this is all really valuable information to have, the downside to Personalysis is that it must be administered and interpreted by a specialist.

Another type of assessment gleans information about a person's style (the D.I.S.C. is one example of this type of test). The best of this type of test that I've encountered is called **Behavior Styles** by the Effectiveness Institute. The test consists of a ten-minute survey of forty or so questions. The way a person makes decisions and responds to others as well as what they need to succeed in a work environment can be determined based on their answers. The test is relatively simple and inexpensive and can give you crucial information needed to make a hiring decision while also providing a blueprint for your working relationship with the person you ultimately hire.

Finally, there are also assessments that measure a person's Emotional Intelligence. I don't recommend using this type of test as a workplace tool. This type of test should only be administered by a trained professional and is not an appropriate assessment for most positions.

One cautionary note: if you decide to use personality assessments with current employees, be sure to provide the proper training to go along with it because friction can result when your people don't understand why you are asking them to take a personality assessment or how you are going to use the information. Sometimes people believe there is a "right" or "wrong" personality, which is one reason I prefer the behavioral assessments like Personalysis. Whatever assessment you choose, make sure your people understand that it is a tool to help them work better and work better together.

Additional Testing and Screening

In addition to the personality profiles or behavior-based inventories, you will most likely want to ask candidates to complete a skills-based assessment as well. For higher-level positions, you can use **Caliper** or another industry-specific assessment. For entry-level positions, depending on the skills required, you might want to administer a Microsoft Office test, or speed or agility tests. For accounting positions, your accountant can probably recommend an appropriate assessment.

As I mentioned earlier, also decide ahead of time if you need to do credit checks, background checks, criminal background checks, or drug tests. If you're using a recruiter, they will sometimes provide these services. If not, you will need to research where to get those services so that you are ready to complete those steps in the final stages of the hiring process.

Verifying Work History and References

As you map out your hiring process, determine how many references you will require and how you will verify those. In our litigious society, most employers are reluctant or unable to give out any more than the standard: "We can verify the dates of employment, the position, and the salary, but nothing more." This protects everyone except you, the potential employer. I once hired an hourly employee I had recruited through an agency. Both the agency and I had checked the candidate's references, yet I ended up having to let her go for some serious indiscretions on her time cards. When I did a little detective work afterward, I found out that all of her references were friends or previous coworkers, not managers. Clearly neither the recruiter nor I had done enough due diligence.

While former employers might be reluctant to give you more than the standard answer, I do always ask: "Would you rehire this person?" It is legal for former employers to answer this question truthfully, and the answer can tell you volumes about the candidate. You can also try to contact someone else in the company. Or ask to talk to a former client or vendor, someone who can affirm that this person has really done what they say they've done. The bottom line is, get proof! For sales people, I've often asked for W-2s to verify earnings. I've heard too many stories from sales people about how they were on quota making big bucks, only to find out after hiring them that they were about to be fired for nonperformance.

If you do get someone on the phone who is willing to talk about the candidate's work performance, always let them know you would only like about five minutes of their time. Ask if that's okay with them. Once they say yes, get them chatting. You'll pick up more than you thought. Only ask questions related to the behavioral traits you're looking for. And be sure to thank them for their help.

If you're hiring someone who is currently employed, verifying current employment can be more difficult because the candidate may not want their employer to know they are interviewing for a new position. Go back to the previous company and check those references. The candidate might also be able to give you the name of someone else at their current company who could at least verify the candidate's position and duties.

Finally, be aware that great performance at a very large corporation or government entity may not translate into a great performance at a smaller firm of one hundred employees. There is inherently more structure at large companies—albeit with varying degrees of functionality—and someone used to that type of environment might have a difficult time translating their skill set successfully to a smaller, more hands-on, or entrepreneurial setting. Again, values and culture matter. Ask candidates about their own, and those of their former employers. Ask references questions about values and culture as well.

At this point, you've screened, tested, interviewed, ranked, and scored all your candidates and should be able to choose which candidate you want to hire. Make the offer! And please, do this in writing. Because conversations can be misunderstood, it's just better for everyone to have the details down on paper.

On-Boarding

By on-boarding I mean what you do to determine the experience your new hires will have their first day on the job. Jack Daly, a Vistage Speaker, talks about how we commemorate a person's retirement, but not when they start. But isn't it just as important to celebrate an employee's introduction to your company? Don't you want them to know that you are truly excited about having them join your group? One of the companies I work with brings balloons, flowers, champagne, and a coffee mug for all employees on their first day. Each new person's cubicle or office is decorated with a big welcome sign and their computer, phone, business cards, and desk are all in order *before* they start. (I know I've started several jobs where I didn't even have a place to sit, and I ended up waiting in the conference room most of the day. Boy did I feel special.) One company I know of even sends flowers or a gift basket home to the spouse of the new employee. How would you feel about your spouse working a few extra hours if you had received this? Probably pretty good.

On the first day, introduce new employees at least to the team they'll be working with, and to as many others in the company as is practical. Take them out to lunch and make the first day really about getting to know them and them getting to know your values and your culture. Those core concepts better be showing on the first day or your new employee will never buy in! Assigning a mentor to help that person navigate through the first day is always a good idea too. This is someone to go to with questions about the company for the first week or so (questions about their specific job would be more appropriate for a manager or a direct coworker).

Whatever you do on the first day, don't make your new employees spend it filling out W-4s and insurance forms. Nothing takes the special out of an experience like bureaucracy. Let your new employees take those forms home to fill out. Spend the first day making sure they feel like they belong.

Thirty, Sixty, and Ninety Day Expectations

Please have these expectations in writing for every position. This is not the same as a probationary period (we'll talk about probationary periods in Chapter Five in detail), so don't use that terminology when discussing expectations. You hired this person for a reason, you have a job description, you have departmental and company goals, and you have an overall strategy you are trying to accomplish. Given all of that, there should be a number of concrete things this person could hope to accomplish within thirty, sixty, and ninety days.

The reason to record and communicate short-term expectations is that you don't yet know your new employee's learning style. They may be a very quick, intuitive learner, and you don't want them to have to wait for you or their manager to tell them what to do next. Short-term expectations let them know what they can move on to independently. Or, your new employee may be a slower, more methodical learner who needs to have the complete picture drawn out in order to accomplish goals. Some people also seem to keep learning steadily as a function of time—each new piece of knowledge builds on the previous piece. Other people are what I've heard called "platform learners," meaning they seem as if they're not getting it at all, and then suddenly they have a huge learning spike and move beyond a peer. Then they'll platform again, and then spike again, and so on. Each position in your company will have different learning requirements, but you will help your people succeed by being understanding of and working with their learning styles.

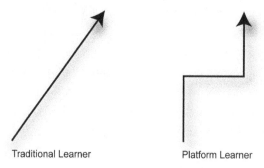

Traditional Learner   Platform Learner

So discuss the goals and objectives for the position with your new hire in the first week, and be sure to answer any questions. Point them in the direction of resources and let them know who to go to for answers. At thirty, sixty, and ninety days have a "debrief" or review, and talk through where they are in accomplishing the goals, and where they need additional help either because they're lagging or because they're leaping ahead. Don't leave them alone just because they are doing great. People who are excelling need to know that, and need to know where to go next. This period is also an opportunity for you to get to know a new employee's communication style to see if it matches any profiles you had done. This is also the time to make any adjustments in working relationships before expectations become entrenched. Be patient but firm about your expectations. The additional time you spend now will pay off dividends in the future. It's certainly cheaper than starting the hiring process all over again!

Don't be afraid to change course here if you discover that this person has talents you didn't see before or if what you thought they had just isn't showing up. Do a reality check and don't be afraid to talk to your new employee about it. Identify the person's strengths and see where you can make them successful within the boundaries of the position. If you have to make an adjustment based on skills and abilities, be sure to document it. Meeting every Monday with the "5 by 5" (a five minute meeting focusing on the five things you want to accomplish) for the week is a great way to document what is and isn't happening.

Reviewing and Measuring Expectations

In addition to reviewing your new hire, the ninety-day period is an opportunity for you to review your hiring process, from job description to job offer. Was what you set out to accomplish with the position reasonable? Did your process for hiring work the way you had hoped? Use both the positives and the negatives from your process review to adjust and refine your next hiring process.

Remember, with hiring, as with marriage, the reason for divorce is always present on the first date! Make sure you are looking for the potential reason for the split and don't let the good feelings blind you to some obvious potential issues.

Additional Resources

Sample Job Description 1

Job Title: VP of Worldwide Sales
Department: Sales
Reports To: CEO

The VP of Worldwide Sales has the overarching responsibility to lead and direct the Widget sales force to meet revenue, profitability, and budgetary objectives. The VP of Worldwide Sales creates and executes the Sales Department's operational strategies in partnership with senior management to achieve business objectives, while maintaining the highest standards of customer support and relationship management.

Essential Duties and Responsibilities

Strategy

- Develop, implement, and manage a progressive worldwide sales strategy that will deliver significant sales growth as projected in the Widget Company strategic plan.
- Develop a worldwide consultant management program including building a contact database, developing resources to serve consultant requirements when building quotes, and penetrating untapped opportunities with consultants to win their loyalty to the Widget product line.
- Participate in corporate planning including forecasting revenue, defining the development queue for new products, and creating strategies for developing business objectives and achieving the company's sales goals.
- Anticipate and react quickly to trends and changes in performance throughout the sales organization.
- Partner with the Director of Marketing to develop lead and revenue generation programs, create effective sales tools, and provide market feedback for marketing campaign development.

Management

- Provide executive team with regular reports on sales department topics and initiatives.

- Facilitate efficient and productive interactions between the sales force and internal business partners including Technical Sales & Support, Manufacturing, Accounting, and Marketing.
- Manage the Sales Department budget.
- Determine and monitor the department's key performance indicators (KPIs) such as revenue vs. plan, contact rate, quote closure rate, and gross profit percentage.
- Develop, document, and enforce sales policies and processes, standard operating procedures, and best practices while streamlining sales activities.
- Set expectations for daily routines and activities for the Sales Department resources, and monitor and measure results; shift strategies to avoid nonproductive activities.
- Maximize the effective use of modern communication technology (e.g., video conferencing) by the sales team in its interaction with business partners, consultants, and customers.
- Travel domestically and internationally for trade show participation, in-person meetings with customers and business partners, and to develop key relationships.
- Set the standard for, and contribute to, a high level of customer satisfaction.
- Hire, supervise, and develop staff and business partners, both internal and external.
- Oversee independent U.S. manufacturer's representatives and international distributors.
- Monitor employee productivity and morale while creating a positive working environment.
- Continually improve the effectiveness of the sales organization and enhance productivity, efficiency, and customer satisfaction.
- Develop and oversee sales training programs for new and existing employees, and ensure sales force is equipped with the products, selling skills, and training required to be successful.
- Define and oversee incentive programs that motivate the sales team to achieve their sales targets.

Required Characteristics

- Detail oriented and organized with strong time-management skills.
- Experience with, and a strong understanding of, the culture of international sales in the widget industry.
- Ability to communicate effectively, both orally and in writing.
- Minimum of five years of experience in a sales leadership role in the widget industry demonstrating the ability to successfully manage a sales force with proven YOY growth of at least 10%.
- Employment history that demonstrates outstanding leadership, communication, and interpersonal skills.
- History of developing successful selling strategies and methodologies, strategic planning and execution, and employee management programs.
- Strong knowledge of the installed widget market, including conferencing.

Desired Characteristics

- Forward thinking with creative ideas.
- Technologically driven, savvy.
- Entrepreneurial mindset.
- Dynamic, outgoing personality.
- Collaborative leadership style.
- Goal and achievement oriented.

Sample Job Description 2

Job Title: Administrative Assistant
Department: Management
Reports To: Business Manager

The Administrative Assistant at the Widget Company is primarily responsi -ble for client services including greeting clients, answering phones, setting appointments, handling client information, and assisting the team to service clients.

Responsibilities

Duties include, but are not limited to:

- Client servicing—greeting clients and all duties associated with front desk and reception responsibilities.
- General office administrative duties—preparation of various client and internal reports, light bookkeeping, marketing and database support, ordering supplies, general office support.
- Administrative Assistant to all Client Advisors and office staff.
- Assist with various projects as needed.

Required Characteristics:

- Minimum of 5 years administrative experience in a professional services firm (Financial services, CPS, Legal or Engineering experience a plus).
- Excellent people skills and positive attitude—genuinely enjoys interfacing with clients and staff.
- Proven track record as team player.
- Self-motivated, proactive, and problem solver.
- Outstanding phone, written, and oral communication skills.
- Detail oriented.
- Strong computer literacy—proficient in MS Office, including database and mail merge functions.
- Ability to multitask, manage deadlines, and succeed under tight deadlines.
- Impeccable ethics, integrity, and honesty.
- Experience with small, quiet office environment.
- Proven ability to keep information confidential.
- Flexible and proactive attitude—volunteers ideas and seeks to solve problems and pitch in where needed.

Desired Characteristics:
- College degree.
- Experience with financial services firm.
- CFP or other financial certification or desire to obtain.

Effective Hiring Through Behavioral Interviewing

Courtesy of the Richmond Group, USA, 2009

What is Behavioral Interviewing?

Behavioral interviewing is a more structured approach to hiring that is based upon the fact that past work behavior is the best predictor of future work performance.

How does Behavioral Interviewing compare to the way most companies interview and hire? Traditional employment interviewing is based upon interviewer bias—the usual "gut feeling" approach to hiring. More emphasis is placed upon whether the candidate is liked than on their natural ability to succeed in the position to be satisfied. The hiring decision is usually made within the first five minutes of the interview with the rest of the interview time spent rationalizing this original impression. This traditional approach helps explain why so many people fail to achieve management's performance expectations. In a Behavioral Interview the hiring manager's foremost goal is to efficiently gather job relevant information that allows for the accurate prediction of future job performance. The primary focus of the interview is to identify past work behaviors. Essentially, good behavioral based interviewing follows the course of scientific investigation; information is received and then analyzed in an organized and consistent manner.

What are the benefits to using Behavioral Interviewing?

There are really many reasons to consider Behavioral Interviewing. To begin with, research has shown that the ability to hire a more effective person is increased by a factor of up to 80 percent. By providing a better match between candidate and job, turnover will decrease and productivity will increase. This more systematic approach to hiring also allows for a fairer selection process less subject to bias and more likely to meet legal guidelines. A better match should lead to greater employee satisfaction and a more positive work environment for managers and employees.

How does a hiring manager prepare to conduct a Behavioral Interview?

To begin, the company or manager must do a careful job analysis of the position to be satisfied. Those behaviors that typify high performance are isolated and used as a basis for developing behavior based questions. As an example, a sales person may be required to show perseverance in a sales situation. Therefore, a related behavioral-based question could be "Please tell me about a recent sale you were involved with where you experienced numerous road blocks." In order to identify these high performance behaviors and related questions a manager should review position descriptions, performance standards, as well as the knowledge, skills, abilities and traits of previous top performers that occupied the position.

How is the interview then conducted?

The manager's goal in the interview is to gather job relevant information that allows for an accurate prediction of future job performance. To achieve this goal each candidate is asked the same pre-developed behavioral-based questions. These questions identify specific previous work related situations, the actions taken by the job candidate in the situation, and the results of these actions. This situation/action/results formula is repeated for each previously identified high performance behavior.

What consideration should a company or manager engage in before embarking upon Behavioral Interviewing?

There are several considerations. First, behavioral-based interviewing does require more skill. One of the keys to success is the redirecting of answers until an appropriate response by the candidate is formulated. This takes practice and sometimes training. Additionally, this technique will require greater discipline, organization and time on the part of the manager conducting the interview. The interviewer will need to be an active listener. Finally, behavioral-based interviewing can be uncomfortable for job candidates. The information they are required to provide can be damaging to their being the ideal candidate. In addition, candidates are not used to this interview style and may struggle with providing behavioral answers versus opinion-based answers to the questions.

Is Behavioral Interviewing only valuable for companies and hiring managers?

Not at all. When companies improve the quality of the match between responsibilities and candidate there is a much greater likelihood of success by the new employee. With greater success comes greater job satisfaction. Additionally, the new employee should not be required to stretch too far from what is natural for them, again creating greater job satisfaction. Candidates for new positions can also employ behavioral-based interviewing to their advantage. By engaging in self-analysis each person can ascertain their strongest most successful behavioral characteristics and those environments they are most likely to succeed in. Behavioral-based questions can then be developed to identify how each opportunity matches their personal high performance environment. As an example, a person may need a more supportive environment and management in order to be most effective. Therefore, a related behavioral-based question could be: "Please tell me about a recent situation where one of your employees was not successful in achieving the goal you had established for them."

What are the standards used to determine good answers to behavioral-based questions?

Good answers will generally have certain commonalties. More recent examples of the desired use of the high performance behavior the more value the response will have. The more closely the example mirrors the task to be performed at the new company the better. Evasive and ambiguous answers may sometimes call for clarification of the question used, but will often mean the person does not have the experience or is not the best candidate for the job. Finally, positive responses are more valuable when confirmed with multiple examples of the high performance behavior.

75 Behavioral Interview Questions To Select The Best Candidate

Courtesy of recruitment startup RecruitLoop's blog (http://recruitloop.com/blog/).

It's a well known fact that looking at a candidate's past behavior is the best way to predict their future performance. So don't waste any more precious interview time asking hypothetical questions. Behavioral interview questions will let you understand in detail how a candidate has acted in specific situations. First, identify the core behaviors you'd like your candidates to demonstrate. Then you can then select your specific questions from the list below. Remember to assess all candidates against the same behavioral criteria!

Ability to Handle Stress

- What has been the most stressful situation you have ever found yourself in at work? How did you handle it?
- What have you done in the past to prevent a situation from becoming too stressful for you or your colleagues to handle?

Adaptability

- Tell me about a situation in which you have had to adjust to changes over which you had no control. How did you handle it?
- Tell me about a time when you had to adjust to a colleague's working style in order to complete a project or achieve your objectives.
- How was your transition from high school to university? Did you face any particular problems? How did you handle them?

Analytical Skills/Problem Solving

- Describe the project or situation that best demonstrates your analytical abilities. What was your role?
- Tell me about a time when you had to analyze information and make a recommendation. What kind of thought process did you go through? Was the recommendation accepted? If not, why?
- Tell me about a situation where you had to solve a difficult problem. What did you do? What was the outcome? What do you wish you had done differently?
- What steps do you follow to study a problem before making a decision? Why?

Attention to Detail

- What process do you use to check that you have the right details from a customer?
- Give me an example of a time you discovered an error that been overlooked by a colleague. What did you do? What was the outcome?
- Tell me about a time that you were confused by a customer's request. What steps did you take to clarify things?

Client Focus/Customer Orientation

- When have you had to deal with an irate customer? What did you do? How did the situation end up?
- Tell me about a time you have "inherited" a customer. What steps did you take to establish rapport with them? What did you do to gain their trust?
- How have you handled a situation in the past where your client has changed the brief or "changed the goalposts"?
- Give an example of a time you went well out of your way to ensure a customer received the best possible service from you and your organisation. What was their reaction?
- When have you ever gone out on a limb to defend a customer? What happened?

Communication

- Tell me about a recent successful experience in making a speech or presentation?
- When have you had to present to a group of people with little or no preparation? What obstacles did you face? How did you handle them?
- Have you ever had to "sell" an idea to your coworkers? How did you do it?
- Give me an example of a time when you were able to successfully communicate with another person even when that individual may not have personally liked you (or vice versa).
- What obstacles or difficulties have you ever faced in communicating your ideas to a manager?
- Tell me about a time in which you had to use your written communication skills in order to get an important point across.

- When have you chosen to communicate a particular message in person as opposed to via email even though the email channel would have been a lot faster?

Creativity

- When was the last time you thought "outside the box" and how did you do it? Why?
- Tell me about a problem that you've solved in a unique or unusual way. What was the outcome? Were you happy or satisfied with it?
- Give me an example of when someone brought you a new idea that was odd or unusual. What did you do?
- When have you brought an innovative idea into your team? How was it received?

Decision Making

- Tell me about a time when you had to make a decision without all the information you needed. How did you handle it?
- Give me an example of a time when you had to be quick in coming to a decision. What obstacles did you face?
- What is the most difficult decision you've ever had to make at work? How did you arrive at your decision? What was the result?
- Give me an example of a business decision you made that you ultimately regretted. What happened?

Goal Setting

- Give me an example of an important career goal which you set yourself and tell me how you reached it. What obstacles did you encounter? How did you overcome the obstacles?
- Tell me about a professional goal that you set that you did not reach. How did it make you feel?
- How have you gone about setting short-term goals and long-term goals for yourself or your team? What steps did you take along the way to keep yourself accountable?

Initiative

- Describe a project or idea (not necessarily your own) that was implemented primarily because of your efforts. What was your role? What was the outcome?

- Describe a situation in which you recognized a potential problem as an opportunity. What did you do? What was the result? What, if anything, do you wish you had done differently?
- Tell me about a project you initiated. What did you do? Why? What was the outcome? Were you happy with the result?
- Tell me about a time when your initiative caused a change to occur.
- What has been the best idea you have come up with during your professional career?

Integrity/Honesty

- Discuss a time when your integrity was challenged. How did you handle it?
- Tell me about a time when you experienced a loss for doing what is right. How did you react?
- Tell me about a business situation when you felt honesty was inappropriate. Why? What did you do?
- Give a specific example of a policy you conformed to with which you did not agree. Why?

Interpersonal Skills

- Give an example of when you had to work with someone who was difficult to get along with. How/why was this person difficult? How did you handle it? How did the relationship progress?
- Describe a situation where you found yourself dealing with someone who didn't like you. How did you handle it?
- Describe a recent unpopular decision you made. How was it received? How did you handle it?
- What, in your opinion, are the key ingredients in guiding and maintaining successful business relationships? Give me examples of how you have made these work for you.
- Give me an example of a time when you were able to successfully communicate with another person even when that individual may not have personally liked you (or vice versa). How did you handle the situation?
- Tell me about a time when you had to work on a team with someone you did not get along with. What happened?

- Describe a situation where you had a conflict with another individual, and how you dealt with it. What was the outcome? How did you feel about it?

Leadership

- Tell me about a team project when you had to take charge of the project? What did you do? What was the result?
- Describe a leadership role of yours outside of work. Why did you commit your time to it? How did you feel about it?
- What is the toughest group that you have ever had to lead? What were the obstacles? How did you handle the situation?
- What has been your greatest leadership achievement in a professional environment? Talk through the steps you took to reach it.
- What have been the greatest obstacles you have faced in building/growing a team?
- Describe a time when you have not only been responsible for leading a team of people but for also doing the same job as your team members? How did you juggle/balance your time?

Planning and Organization/Time Management

- Describe a situation that required you to do a number of things at the same time. How did you handle it? What was the result?
- How do you prioritize projects and tasks when scheduling your time? Give me some examples.
- Tell me about a project that you planned. How did your organize and schedule the tasks? Tell me about your action plan.
- When has a project or event you organised not gone according to plan? What happened? Why? How did you feel?

Sales/Negotiation

- Tell me about your previous success in building a customer base from a standing start. What steps did you take?
- What is your greatest sales-related achievement to date? What steps led to the final outcome?
- Describe a time when you convinced a resistant customer to utilize your services.
- What was the most stressful professional negotiation you have been involved in? How did you handle it?

Teamwork

- Describe a situation where others you were working with on a project disagreed with your ideas. What did you do?
- Tell me about a time when you worked with a colleague who was not doing their share of the work. How did you handle it?
- Describe a situation in which you had to arrive at a compromise or help others to compromise. What was your role? What steps did you take? What was the result?
- Tell me about a time when you had to work on a team that did not get along. What happened? What role did you take? What was the result?
- What was the biggest mistake you have made when delegating work as part of a team project?
- Tell me about a time when you had settle a dispute between team members. How did you go about identifying the issues? What was the result?
- What have you found to be the difficult part of being a member, not leader, of a team? How did you handle this?

Tenacity/Resilience

- Tell me about a particular work-related setback you have faced. How did you deal with it?
- When have you ever found yourself in a competitive situation professionally? How did you handle it?
- When have you seen your tenacity or resilience really pay off in a professional setting? What was the outcome?

Sample Interview Questions for a Business Development Associate

Values we are looking for:

Kindness, caring, commitment.

Behavioral characteristics we are looking for:

Self directed, friendly, goal driven, outgoing, hard working, communication skills, organization.

Questions:

- Tell me about a time when you had to get a job done with little or no direction. How did you do it? How did it feel?
- Describe for me a time when you went to a function and you didn't know anyone. What did you do?
- How have you used goals in your life, both personally and professionally? How does that show up in your every day life?
- Tell me about a time when the amount of time allotted wasn't enough and something just had to get done. What did you do?
- Describe some of the commitments in your life currently. What do those mean to you?
- Tell me about your favorite boss. Why was that person your favorite? How did he or she treat you? What about your worst boss? What was the difference?
- How do you like to be communicated with? Tell me about a time when you had a big miscommunication with someone? What was the outcome?
- What excites you about this position? Why?
- How would you describe your organizational ability? What does your desk look like? How does it work for you?
- What was the best working environment you ever had? Why?

You may not get through all the questions. Drill down with each one to find out what the candidate really thinks. Try to get the person to give specific examples not just descriptions of what they thought or how they felt.

Sample Performance Review Worksheet

Name:

Date:

Goals for Quarter

Set specific goals, at least three business and one personal.

1.
2.
3.
4.
5.
6.

Accomplishments Towards Goals

Address each of the goals listed above and note any progress or accomplishments.

1.
2.
3.
4.
5.
6.

Disappointments

Identify anything that was not accomplished or did not work out.

Insights Gained

What was learned from this? Were there any "Aha!" moments?

Stop, Start, Continue

What will employee stop doing, start doing, or continue doing to accomplish goals, or to grow both personally and professionally.

Hiring Checklist

- ☐ List the positions you need to fill to make your one-year vision happen.
- ☐ Using the models earlier in this chapter write a brief job description for each position.
- ☐ For each position, list the required and desired skills and experience.
- ☐ For each position, list the required and desired behavioral traits.
- ☐ Conduct research on salary ranges for each position. Set a base salary that is at the top end of the range.
- ☐ Decide whether you will recruit using internal or external resources.
- ☐ Decide on your resume-ranking process.
- ☐ Choose a candidate prescreener.
- ☐ Compose three prescreening questions.
- ☐ Choose your interviewing team.
- ☐ Set three interview times and places.
- ☐ Write ten behavior-based interview questions.
- ☐ Decide on any additional questions you will need to ask.
- ☐ Decide on your candidate-ranking process.
- ☐ List any additional assessments you will require.
- ☐ Decide how you will verify work histories.
- ☐ Describe the on-boarding process for each position.
- ☐ Describe your short-term expectations and goals for each position.
- ☐ Describe how and when you will assess your hiring process.

Recommended Reading

Now, Discover Your Strengths, Marcus Buckingham and Donald O. Clifton, Free Press, 2001.

Puzzle Piece Five
HR and Your Employee Handbook

In most organizations, human resources is the department within the organization that supports your most valuable resource: all things "human." Companies with fewer than fifty employees frequently delegate this to the Controller, Office Manager, or whichever manager says, "Yes, I'm good with people." In this type of situation, "HR" usually means the person who takes care of the required paperwork for employees.

If we agree that the most expensive, complicated to find, and difficult to replace resource is your people, why don't most entrepreneurs make human resources more of a priority? I believe it's because most leaders think they're not good at HR and are afraid they'll make mistakes, possibly costly ones. Sometimes they're afraid of being sued, sometimes that they don't know how to manage people, sometimes of conflict, and generally (like most people) of what they don't know. But I recommend that you make "human resources" one of your top priorities as a CEO. Don't let this one just fall into someone's lap. Intentionally find your most skilled and knowledgeable "people" person to be in charge of HR. Otherwise, you might just find out why there are so many good employment attorneys in practice.

Once your company gets to a certain size (usually at about fifty to seventy-five people), and depending on the nature of your business, you'll need a full-time HR professional. Up to that point, the duty can be shared with another position, but it's always advisable to enlist outside help in addition to your internal person. Following are some of the issues, including an employee handbook, that your HR person or team will want to consider to keep your employees satisfied and your company productive.

HR Duties

Once you've designated the lead for your HR functions, it's important that you're both clear on what that person will be responsible for in that role. Following is a list of some of the duties your HR head is likely to be in charge of:

- Job descriptions
- Salary ranges
- Recruiting
- Interviewing
- Hiring
- Training
- Firing
- Company policies
- Benefits contact
- Handbook
- Enforcement
- Company morale

This is just a short list of possible duties of the HR professional in your company. Just be clear about that person's level of authority—where it begins and ends—and what the responsibilities of the position are.

HR Team

In most companies too small for a full-time HR professional, these duties will likely be shared amongst several executives or managers. Be sure to match duties to both skills and personalities. For example, if you have an intuitive manager who is particularly good at reading people, put that person on the interviewing team. (On the other hand, having someone on your HR team who enjoys firing people will most likely lead to lawsuits. In HR, regardless of wrongdoing, you will always have to prove you were not at fault, and doing so will most often be expensive.) Because people like to be involved in the decisions that directly affect them, make sure you have different departments represented including the one where the position is open. However, be clear about the authority you grant these individuals. Are you asking for input or a decision? Not making this type of expectation clear from the outset could leave your people feeling that their input was not heard or valued.

Outside Resources

For smaller companies, there are several organizations that can function as your employer's HR resource. In Washington State we have an organization called Washington Employers, Inc. which acts as an outside HR resource for companies in Washington State. A company like this is invaluable because they will review your handbook, answer legal questions, and recommend other kinds of outside help when you need it.

There are usually two other types of outside help: 1.) an employment attorney who is an expert in your state's employment laws; or 2.) some type of coach, counselor, mediator, or other employment professional who can help before a situation escalates to the attorney level. The latter type of help can be invaluable because it can be difficult to determine which stage you're at when a situation is getting complicated. Because state and federal governments almost always side with the employee, it's wise to get help early and often.

When you do need to hire an attorney, don't make the mistake of going to your business attorney for advice on employment matters. These areas of expertise are quite different, so go straight to the right kind of expert. Employment attorneys come in two varieties: ones who represent employers and ones who represent employees. When you choose an employment attorney, make sure yours has experience successfully representing employers.

Here's an example of how a situation can get out of hand despite good intentions. I once had a sales employee who stopped coming to work due to "medical problems." We granted him extra vacation and paid for it as a kindness. Then we let him take an extended leave of absence for two months. When he returned, we found out that he had voluntarily gone for electroshock therapy (an extreme treatment for depression). We could no longer let him work the phone with customers because he was not coherent or consistent when speaking. We offered him several other positions, which he declined, so we had no choice but to offer him unemployment and lay him off. The next day we were served with a wrongful termination suit from the state. Although we won the first round, he went on to file a civil suit which we ended up settling. We later found out that he had run up all his credit cards in the preceding month and had filed for bankruptcy the same day he sued us. We devoted considerable resources, including some significant out of pocket costs, to dealing with this situation.

There are several lessons to learn from the above experience. First, paying for the extra vacation set a very costly precedent for other employees. We might have averted this issue by having the policy spelled out more clearly in our employee handbook (which I'll talk about in depth shortly). Second, not getting better legal advice at the first hint of trouble cost us tens of thousands of dollars. So don't keep throwing Band-Aids on an employee problem like we did. Get the outside help you need early.

Employee Surveys

Your employees are a great source of information about how your company is doing, both internally and externally. Remember, your job is to grow your people. As the CEO, you want to know what your employees think and feel about your organization so you can do just that. One way to do this is with surveys. There are more expensive surveys you can outsource to HR firms to find out what's "really going on" and you will glean some good information from these. They are usually anonymous and ask general questions about how employees are treated and how they're feeling. However, some employees don't believe they're anonymous, and therefore are not truthful about anything they fear might lead to retribution or punishment. And that's probably the information you most need to know.

One of the best, and least expensive, ways to survey your employees is to use the "Twelve Questions" model developed by Marcus Buckingham in his book *First, Break all the Rules: What the World's Greatest Managers Do Differently*. This short survey asks twelve simple questions that tell you a lot about how your employees feel about working for you. The beauty of this survey model is that it's easy to administer, easy to take, and nonthreatening. (You can easily find the survey online by searching for the "Gallup Q12.")

Typically, it's enough to survey your employees once a year. However, if you're implementing a major change initiative, are making a change in ownership or management, or are undergoing any other significant event you might want to survey more frequently.

Two Cautionary Notes on Surveys

Cautionary Note 1: If there is some obvious deficiency or action that should be addressed as a result of the survey, *be sure to take action.* Communicate what you will be doing, when, how, and why. There will be an exponentially greater negative impact for doing nothing after asking for input, than for asking for nothing and doing nothing. Always communicate what you found out and what you are going to do about it.

Cautionary Note 2: Always have your most trusted individual (usually the HR Director or Manager) oversee the survey and review the results so employees never feel they can't be honest about a manager for fear of retribution. Once you've lost your employees' trust that they can speak honestly you can never gain it back.

Performance Reviews

While performance reviews can provide valuable feedback and coaching to an employee, most do not. The keys to a good performance review are consistency, brevity, clarity, and a mutual agreement on the plan going forward. Let's go over each of these points in more depth.

Consistency means that, whatever policy you have for timing of reviews, follow it. If you're going to change the timing for whatever reason, make it known well in advance. If you don't, your employees will tell their own stories about why you aren't doing reviews, and their interpretations will almost always be wrong and negative.

I prefer to do reviews quarterly or semiannually. An annual performance review is a year late, and will tend to focus on one or two good and bad things without really giving accurate and timely feedback to the employee about what you want. A quarterly review provides for timely feedback so that course corrections can be made if necessary. Conduct reviews in the spirit of coaching. This is an opportunity for you to grow your employees through mentoring. They shouldn't feel like they're visiting the principal's office.

Brevity means make reviews short (fifteen to thirty minutes at the most) and to the point. Don't go through a long laundry list of personality characteristics that will be graded on a scale of one to five. Realistically that has no impact on the work you need this person to execute in the near future. Instead focus on goals that you mutually set at the beginning of the year, semiannually, or quarterly.

The first time you do performance reviews, sit down with your employees and guide them through goal setting, and what you think will help their careers, the company, and the position or department they're in.

The second time you do this have employees submit their reviews to you in advance, at least one week prior to your scheduled meeting. Make notes or add comments to their reviews on the same form, and then discuss their comments and yours at the assigned review time. Setting this up as a conversation, not an inquisition, will promote trust and growth.

Remember that the key to any behavioral change—which is the only kind of change you can really affect at work—is timely and consistent feedback and coaching. The same principal applies for recognizing desirable behavior: good employees want to know that they're on the right track and that you appreciate what they're doing. If they work in a feedback vacuum, they'll likely stop performing well or they'll go elsewhere.

Clarity means that when you leave the performance review (coaching session), each of you is crystal clear on the objectives, what was meant by what was said, and the plan for moving forward. Don't leave the meeting until you're sure your employee understands all feedback and goals, and doesn't have any lingering questions or thoughts. It's important that your people feel heard.

Mutual agreement fosters buy-in so your employees are really invested in their own growth and development. If you're doing performance reviews only to get better performances out of people, forget it. Your people need to know that you're concerned about their well-being and their personal growth. The benefit to you is that employees who feel like they're growing will help your company grow. Let your people participate in setting their goals, or even let them come up with the performance goals. In most cases where I've seen employers implement this type of goal setting, the employees are much more aggressive than their leaders. It might seem easier just to assign goals, but using goal-setting as an opportunity to negotiate and discuss why certain targets are mutually beneficial to the company *and* the employee has long-term payoffs that dictating objectives never does.

By implementing a methodology of more frequent, brief reviews, you have two to four evaluations in place when it's time to look at raises. When you look back at those documented reviews, it's not a mystery to anyone whether your mutually agreed upon goals have been met. If you've been clear and concise with your goals there should be no ambiguity about achievement, and the discussion about raises should be fairly simple.

That said, I'm a believer in decoupling pay raises from performance reviews. Every company should have a fair pay policy such that, as long as both individual and company goals are met, an annual, fair, wage increase should be given (usually 2–7%). For exceptional performance, however (a project that was pulled from the fire and rescued, outstanding leadership, etc.), an additional bonus should be awarded.

Once again, though, use your values to guide your pay practices. Is the way you pay your employees consistent with who you are? Are people rewarded fairly for performance? Do you have other incentives (time off, vacations, etc.) that also reward good employees? Make sure you develop a combination of incentives so that the work and the incentive aren't always about pay.

To reiterate the basic principles of performance reviews: be consistent, brief, clear, and in agreement. You'll be happy you did. (See the Sample Performance Review Form at the end of Chapter Four.)

Fostering Collaboration

Let me preface this by saying that collaboration is not as important in some companies as in others, and in some it's not important at all. For example, some outside consulting firms might not care if their people work together productively, because collaboration isn't a requirement for success as a consultant. However, in most cases, some sort of collaboration is necessary to achieve company goals. You as the leader, in conjunction with your managers, need to determine how much interaction is necessary. So, once you're clear on where you're headed and what you hope to accomplish, diagram out where each of your departments intersect, and devise ways that they can be incentivized to work together. Think of this as intentional collaboration.

Why is *intentional* collaboration important? Because, when goals and incentives are not interrelated, inter-departmental collaboration is unlikely to be present. While competition within a company can be a great motivator, if it is at cross-purposes with collaboration—and therefore the company's overall goals—you are creating waste in both human potential and material resources. For instance, an outside sales team that needs the customer service department to deliver as promised will need to find ways to work together. If the two teams see themselves as competitors, no collaboration can happen. Instead, pair them up to achieve the mutual goal of customer satisfaction so they support one another. Sales and service teams that have mutual goals usually perform to higher standards with happier customers as a result.

A very successful engineering firm had a problem with delivery dates, leaving the sales team constantly over-promising and the service team under-delivering. This caused each team to point fingers at one another. The CEO sat down with both department heads and facilitated a discussion that lead to an agreement about mutual goals. Both sides acknowledged behaviors that were not serving the ultimate goal of promoting new products, and they devised ways they could work together versus working from separate agendas. The result was a clear communication process, no more in-fighting or hidden agendas, and two departments that celebrated each other's successes so mutual goals could be met. It was the first year in which each of these two departments not only met, but exceeded, the company's goals.

Gaining collaboration is usually pretty simple. It's just a matter of acknowledging what is currently happening, how that is at cross-purposes with the company's values, and what it's costing the company in time and money. Once the wrong road is identified, it's easier for everyone to move to the right track. So, decide which areas of your company absolutely need collaboration and how you will foster it with teams, rewards, incentives, and shared goals. Also decide what you'll do when collaboration gets off track. Having a plan will make it easier to identify and rectify a collaboration snag when it happens.

Celebrating the Wins

Winning teams love to celebrate. We've all been involved with companies that have "employee of the year" awards or other annual rewards. Whether or not these are actually rewarding and motivating depends on how the recipients are chosen and the awards administered. A big part of making rewards successful is rewarding what deserves to be rewarded. You'll need to decide, consistent with your vision and culture, what is part of someone's job (the minimum they have to do to get paid) and what is something more that deserves recognition. This can be a very fine line. If you recognize an "employee of the month" and one month you give it to someone simply because they haven't ever received it or because no one else really did anything outstanding, you've just gutted the value of the award. If one of your values is integrity or authenticity, and you do this, you have now violated a core value. Much better not to give the award when no one has actually earned it.

One program I've seen work successfully is a rewards program where employees hand out tickets to each other for whatever it is you want to encourage (this is sometimes called a "WOW" program). Each month, the employee with the most tickets gets half a day off. This can be a very inexpensive and effective motivational program that also builds awareness and good will amongst your employees. You could even tailor this around your company values, where employees could give out tickets every time someone did an outstanding job living the company values (they should all already be living them, so make sure it's above and beyond).

However you choose to celebrate wins, start by determining what's most important to your employees and develop the program around that. Remember that one size doesn't fit all. For example, a design firm chose to reward hours completed on time for each contract. Each designer was awarded hours that accrued on a chart all year. Anyone who reached a certain number of on-time billable hours (meaning within the project scope and deadlines) could earn a trip to Italy. The company made a huge chart with planes and destinations to put in the conference room so they had a visual at all times of where everyone was on their "journey." Some employees complained that they didn't have as many opportunities to earn hours as others, to which the CEO responded: "Make yourself an opportunity." And they did. The majority of the team was able to earn the trip. While the contest aspect rewarded individual performance, the company acknowledged the importance of the team by inviting everyone who didn't earn the trip to go at their own expense. Some did.

My favorite incentive was by a Seattle manufacturer and distributor of tchotchkes. After the company had achieved an incredible sales hurdle—a real stretch goal—the CEO decided to reward everyone in the company. He chartered two buses and drove all the employees to the mall. Once there, he gave them each $200 in cash. The rules were: they had one hour to spend it; they could not spend it on someone else; and they couldn't save it. After an hour everyone boarded the buses and returned to the office where they showed their items and told why they had bought them. Afterward, they had a pizza party. This adventure did so much for company spirit during a difficult time that it became an annual event that produced great results in both morale and productivity. Not surprisingly, one of this company's values was fun, which they certainly demonstrated through this exercise.

To sum up, the key to success with any reward program is that it contain the following elements:

- The reward is appropriate to the desired behavior.
- The program rewards both individual and team goals.
- The rewards are in alignment with company values.
- The behavior being rewarded is in alignment with overall company goals.
- The program is clearly defined and measurable.
- The program changes so it doesn't lose value.
- The program is not set up as a popularity contest.
- There are both structured and random elements.
- Families are included in annual programs because your employees need support from home to give extra hours.
- The recognition feels positive to the individual employee (not everyone likes to get up in front of a crowd).
- The program is creative, visible, and fun!

Employee Handbook

This should be the guidebook for everything employee related within your company. There are numerous samples and templates available to you to create an employee handbook, but the cautionary words are *less is more*. The more complex your handbook is, the more rigidly you'll have to handle all situations and, consequently, the more things you can potentially be sued for. The less you have specifically identified, the more freedom you'll have to use common sense. Like me, you might have wondered how big corporations, unions, and governments create employees who are incompetent (think of the DMV) and in a lot of cases downright scary (think of the U.S. Postal Service). The simple answer is *too many rules*. Too many rules takes the power to think away from your employees and makes them dependent on structure. From a management perspective, the more rules you have, the harder it is to fire someone legally.

Once you've decided on the source of your template or hired someone to write your handbook, you will also need to find a third party to review it. At its most basic, your HR manual should accurately reflect all of your company policies. But it should also include three additional elements: adherence to current law, enforceability, and, most importantly, common sense. Your employee handbook should start out with a company history so that how you started and what you have been working on are recorded somewhere. This also gives your new employees a little window into what the company has done. Your handbook is also a good place to reinforce your intentional purpose: your mission, vision, and values (those three statements you worked so hard on). If you do so nowhere else in your company, you should have those things recorded here. Of course, by this point, I hope you have them in many more places than just your handbook!

A note of caution before you start: as you develop your manual be careful to use the word "behavior" instead of "attitude." Behavior is concrete and observable, while "attitude" is very subjective and interpretive. In the event that you need to fire someone, you'll be on much firmer ground pointing to specific behaviors.

Employment Practices: What You Need to Spell Out

Equal Employment Opportunity

Yes, you do need to say that you are an equal employment opportunity employer. If you don't, you just open yourself up to potential lawsuits. The statement doesn't need to say that you embrace the world, but it must say that you do not discriminate and that you adhere to all federal and state laws relating to such and to the Americans with Disabilities Act (ADA), and that you communicate employee rights as required by law.

Harassment and Anti-Discrimination

The purpose of this statement is to help create a workplace that is free from all forms of harassment, and to insist that all employees are treated with respect, dignity, and courtesy. This should make very clear what the company stance is against harassment and discrimination and what the complaint procedure is. You should also include some examples of unacceptable behavior and the consequences of such conduct. See the sample harassment and anti-discrimination statement at the end of this chapter.

At Will Status

This is where a lot of small employers get confused. "At will status" simply means that you can let people go when you want to because they are employed "at will." Most, but not all, states include "at will" in their employment regulations. Basically then, the fact that you hired someone doesn't mean you have an obligation to keep them employed (this may not be true if you have signed a contract), though it doesn't mean you can treat them unfairly. I encourage you to always do your best to make a place for someone, but if that person really doesn't fit into your organization, you can let them go. Where companies get into trouble is when they negate their "at will" status by using terms such as "probationary period," "trial period," "cause," "permanent," "career," and "loyalty." All of these words are problematic because they imply that, if an employee does perform any kind of paid work for your company, he or she will be entitled to permanent employment. For this reason alone, you need to have this section of your employee handbook reviewed by an outside expert to keep you safe.

Attendance and Leave Policies

This is simply the place in your handbook where you identify what constitutes acceptable attendance for your company. It could be something like this:

The Widget Company commits to customers to meet certain work schedules and delivery dates. In order to do this, we must be able to depend on regular attendance of all our employees. We look on regular attendance as an essential requirement of any job.

And then you would go on to explain what your rules are regarding tardiness and absenteeism: specifically, what is and isn't acceptable; who employees have to report to and by when; whether or not they have to cover their shift; when they need to have a doctor's note (usually after three days); and what happens if they don't follow the rules. If you have over fifty employees, you'll need to identify that they are covered under the Family Medical Leave Act and explain what that means for them.

Think about whether there are other types of leave you will accept in addition to those dictated by law. Sabbaticals are a great way to retain excellent employees by giving them an opportunity to recharge. In our overworked society, creative leave policies can be a great non pay-based incentive.

Overtime and Work Schedule Policies

If your company has regular work schedules or potential for overtime, you need to define that in your Employee Handbook. I won't go into all the possible rules for overtime here; suffice it to say that, if you have hourly employees (these are referred to as "nonexempt employees") and you adhere to the standard forty-hour week, you will need to pay overtime and time-and-a-half if they work more than forty hours. However, there are all sorts of rules relating to the "work period" and how you calculate overtime (for example, if nonworked paid time counts towards the forty hours). You will need to decide what you will pay and what you won't according to federal and state laws and then put it in writing.

Salaried employees (referred to as "exempt employees") are not entitled to overtime (presumably this is because they are generally paid more than hourly workers). The theory is that salaried employees do their job until they are done and you do not count hours. This is where you need to be very careful with any compensation for "extra" hours worked because any attempt to compensate salaried employees for additional hours will put them into the nonexempt category. I do not recommend using "comp time" for employees who work more than expected as it could be construed as being owed to them as overtime or pay for this work. The CEO of a design firm I worked with got into serious trouble with the labor department by "requiring" a certain number of hours from her junior designers. Since the hours were counted, she had to go back for two years and pay overtime for all hours that were recorded in employee files on time sheets. A very costly mistake. These rules and others are defined by the Fair Labor Standards Act.

Fair Labor Standards Act (FLSA)

The FLSA sets minimum hourly wages, training wages, overtime hours and rates, and regulates the employment of children under eighteen. If state and federal laws conflict, employers must follow the one most favorable to the employee.

Substance Abuse and Workplace Violence Policies

Although it seems like common sense that, due to potential risk, you don't tolerate the abuse of any drugs, legal or illegal, at work, you do actually have to say it. You also need to identify your remedy for it (warnings, termination, counseling, outpatient treatment, etc.)

And of course you don't tolerate violence, but it will come up so decide how you'll deal with it now and put that in your employee handbook. I once had an employee come to work drunk after calling in sick and then promptly pick a fight with another employee. As far as I was concerned he'd hit the trifecta (abuse of sick leave, alcohol abuse at work, violence at work) and I fired him. But you might be surprised that his manager wanted to keep him on because he was "such a good worker." Had the rules for all three of those offenses not been spelled out in our handbook, the manager would have tried to get me to relent and keep the employee on. Remember, what you're willing to tolerate is part of your culture, so be very careful when setting your policies.

Company Rules

Company rules are interesting because they are the list of things you absolutely will not tolerate. These are the things that are first offense causes for firing. I've also seen this called the company "code of conduct" or "rules of conduct." Interestingly, being fired for breaking an expressed rule is the one circumstance in which our state Employment Security Department will deny unemployment benefits. You can let someone go for all sorts of good reasons but, unless they break a rule, they will most likely be eligible for unemployment or more.

Things you will likely include in your rules are:

- Theft or inappropriate removal or possession of property of the Company or others
- Falsification of timekeeping records
- Working under the influence of alcohol or illegal drugs
- Possession, distribution, sale, transfer, or use of alcohol or illegal drugs in the workplace
- Fighting or threatening violence in the workplace
- Boisterous or disruptive activity in the workplace
- Negligence or improper conduct leading to damage of Company-owned, customer-owned, or coworker-owned property
- Insubordination or other disrespectful conduct
- Violation of safety or health rules
- Sexual or other unlawful or unwelcomed harassment
- Discrimination
- Excessive absenteeism or any absence without notice
- Excessive tardiness or leaving work without permission
- Unauthorized use of telephones, or other Company-owned equipment
- Using Company equipment for purposes other than business (i.e. playing games on computers or personal Internet usage)
- Unauthorized disclosure of business "secrets" or confidential information
- Violation of personnel policies
- Unsatisfactory performance or conduct

These are just a few sample rules. You can add as many as you like, but just make sure you are clear that violating any of the items on this list will lead to immediate termination. (The above rules are from a sample employee handbook courtesy of Stonetrust Commercial Insurance Company.)

Disciplinary Process and Terminations

In this area of your handbook, you'll address what remedy an employee has if they are unhappy with their supervisor or manager. You'll want to spell out the steps they should take to make the issue visible without fear of retribution.

This is also the place where you'll lay out the way someone's behavior will be addressed in the event that it is out of standard. Typically you'll use a three-part process: verbal warning, written warning, termination. This way the department of labor sees that you have made an effort to allow the employee to correct the behavior. This is one of those areas where you want to specifically avoid using the word "probation." The reason for this is that you want to retain the ability to terminate that person at any time in the future for a similar infraction. If you use the word "probation" in your verbal or written disciplinary process, you are implying that, after they successfully complete whatever the "probationary" time period is without demonstrating the problem behavior, they are not subject to termination in the future for reoccurrence of the same behavior. In effect, the slate is erased after the probationary period of time.

Let's examine the steps in a disciplinary process in more detail:

Step One: Verbal Warning

You'll have a verbal conversation with the employee and ask for the behavior to be corrected. Be sure to also keep a written record of this conversation including the date, time, and what was said.

Step Two: Written Warning

You'll describe the behavior in writing, and also describe what needs to happen by when, and what will happen if it doesn't. This is a good place to use the phrase: "Consequences for an additional infraction include further disciplinary action, up to and including termination."

Step Three: Termination

When you have to terminate someone, please do so with the utmost respect for that individual as a human being. So often we get wrapped up in our emotions and feel vindicated by a termination, only to have it haunt us with further threats of litigation or unemployment. Decide if you're willing to give the employee a severance package. One week for every year employed is typical; one month for every year if it's a higher-level executive. Of course, get a release of further action if you do give them a severance package.

Don't worry too much about unemployment if you fire someone. As I said earlier, unless someone broke a stated company rule, that person is likely to get unemployment benefits. Yes, it will affect your rating, but in the long run, it's cheaper than litigation.

Company Benefits

These are all the things you offer your employees besides salary. They can really make a difference when recruiting because they are often more important for employees than money. You don't need to go overboard, but do determine what is standard for your industry, and then make yours just a little bit better. Most importantly, figure out what benefits reflect and reinforce your unique culture. Don't be afraid to be creative!

For all benefits you'll need to decide the following:

- When does it start accruing?
- Do employees lose it if they don't use it within a given period?
- Does it get paid out at the end of each year, upon termination, or on some other schedule?
- When are employees eligible to participate?
- Under what circumstances do benefits change?

The best gauge I know for what you're willing to give is what I call the "resentment test." What benefits are you willing to give and not be resentful about? When you hit the resentment threshold, you've got the right number or policy.

Vacation

What are you willing to offer for vacation? Two weeks per year to start is standard, and it can go up from there. You'll also need to decide if executives have a different standard than other employees or if everyone's vacation will be the same. Also think about what you can do to encourage employees to use vacation so that they come back refreshed and ready to work. And what can you do to make sure they don't dread vacation because of the mountain of work that piles up while they're gone?

Sick Time

Sick benefits are tricky. One company I worked with had twelve annual sick days, but, if you used them, it was reflected in your year-end bonus. As a result people came to work sick and made the healthy employees sick. There were others who used up their sick time and everyone knew they weren't sick, but the CEO wouldn't change the policy because "that's the way it was." Consequently, this was always a contentious issue among employees and caused a lot of needless conversation and angry feelings. One remedy might be to declare that, after three days, people need a doctor's note. On the other hand, just about anyone can get a doctor's note to say they're sick. And do you really want to be in the business of checking up on your employees?

Personal Time Off (PTO)

This is the solution I prefer to the sick leave conundrum. Personal Time Off or Paid Time Off is just that: time when the employee is not at work for whatever reason. Most large organizations have gone to this type of policy because it takes them out of the police business. Vacation and Sick time are combined into a single leave package for employees to use as they please. I've also seen holidays and other types of time off rolled into PTO as well.

If you go this route, you'll have to decide how many days and how you'll pay it out if someone leaves your company. Sometimes, with PTO that includes sick pay, leave is not paid out in full when an employee departs, but that is a decision you'll have to make in accordance with your company's values.

Holidays

What holidays will you pay out? The typical holiday list includes six, but some organizations (government and banks) include up to twelve, which can be attractive to employees. Standard holidays include:

- Christmas
- New Year's Day
- Thanksgiving
- Labor Day

- Memorial Day
- Fourth of July

Optional holidays include:

- Christmas Eve
- President's Day
- Day after Thanksgiving
- MLK Day
- New Year's Eve

Other Time Off

This includes such things as bereavement, jury duty, family leave, prolonged sickness, and sabbaticals. Again, be clear on your policy here or roll all of those into PTO. Doing this would let you avoid having to deal with the employee who wanted to use bereavement leave when his hamster died. However you decide to do this, make sure it is very clear from the start so you can avoid potential minefields (like a disagreement about what constitutes bereavement) where you are never going to be the nice guy.

Insurance

You should align yourself with a good broker or insurance company that can offer a competitive package to employees. Generally speaking, the larger your company, the more competitive you can be with this package, but again, make sure it's in alignment with your values. If you're a smaller company and can't afford a rich benefits package, offer a flex plan or cafeteria plan that you put pretax money into for medical benefits. Even if you're small, try to find some way to help employees out.

Auto

Make sure you have a clear auto policy if you have employees who use either their own cars or company vehicles for work. If employees use their own cars, they will need to carry their own insurance and you'll need to see a copy of their policy, but you'll also need to compensate them for the wear and tear on their car. The easiest way to calculate an auto allowance is simply to give employees a flat rate. For example, you might allot $500 a month, or more or less depending on the amount of driving and the type of car. Or you can simply reimburse for mileage after the employee submits an expense report. I've seen several cases of "creative" expense reports when it comes to mileage, so, if you don't want to get into the "spy" business, just go with an allowance. Check with your accountant to be sure you're doing this correctly and withholding tax if applicable.

Reimbursements

Decide how you'll reimburse your employees for expenses. Make sure the system is easy to follow and put it in writing. That way, if an employee says his dog ate the receipts, you can simply point to the policy that says that, in order to be reimbursed, employees must submit receipts.

401K/Retirement

Even if your business is too small to contribute to a 401K or pension plan of some sort, you can set one up so that your employees can contribute themselves. It's a good idea to help employees with savings and this gives them an avenue to do so.

Employee Assistance Program

This is an outside service that can provide assistance to employees when they're having personal problems at home or sometimes at work. You usually pay a fee per employee and then employees have a resource to go to when they're in trouble. Employee assistance programs are usually confidential unless there's a potential risk to the business. If the employee needs ongoing counseling, they'll be referred to another provider, usually at the employee's expense.

Company Property and Privacy Policies

These are all the policies that will protect you when employees use company equipment. Basically you want to define how employees are to use anything the company owns and what happens if the policy is violated. This is one part of the handbook you really want to make sure your employees understand. Have your employees acknowledge that they understand this policy and also print it as a separate form that you post visibly in several places.

Internet

We've all heard stories or had experience with an employee who spends hours surfing the net instead of working. Today there are all sorts of very sophisticated software products available to companies who want either to prevent employees from using the Internet or to monitor how they use it. In most cases these are good for you because they protect you from liability in the event an employee does something wrong or illegal while using your equipment. First, decide which employees need to use computers, and then decide which sort of software you need to install for prevention or monitoring. Make sure employees know you are monitoring their computer use and put the policy in writing. A local hospital installed prevention software on computers in the doctor's lounge without notifying employees. Several doctors then complained that something was wrong with the computers because suddenly they weren't able to access all the sites they used to. As it turned out, those were the computers that some doctors were using to access adult content. Who knew.

Computers

Computers are the property of the company and therefore you are liable if they are used inappropriately. For this reason, I recommend that employees be aware that you can track and record anything they do on company computers and make sure they have no expectation of privacy. Some will say that, while they are on break or off hours, they should be able to do what they want but I disagree. You just don't want to be responsible for non work-related activity on your equipment period.

Voicemail

As with computers, there should be no expectation of privacy on company phones and voicemail.

Email and Texting

This one gets everyone in trouble. Think about General Patraeus. The easiest way to deal with the cascade of private emails coming in to work is to state that work email addresses are not for personal use and will be monitored. This will encourage employees to use a personal address. But do remind employees that personal email addresses accessed on work computers can also be tracked so that is not private either.

You should also address whether or not you allow instant messaging or texting on work as well as personal devices. This can be very distracting during a workday and, in most cases, is not necessary.

Other Property

Define what is and isn't work property. In most cases it's everything at the place of business, but you'd be surprised what I've seen go home. I caught one employee putting an oversized monitor in his car. His reasoning? The employee that had previously used it was let go and he knew we weren't replacing that person, so he thought the monitor was an extra. Yeah right.

Confidentiality

This is simply a statement that all work created at your place of business is the property of your business and that all trade secrets, ideas, patents, company secrets, or information is to be kept within the company, and you'll take action if information ends up where it shouldn't. In most cases, you want employees to sign these "nondisclosures" and "noncompetes" when they start with you. This is because most courts will disallow them if employees sign them after starting and are not given proper compensation. I worked with one CEO who decided that all employees should sign noncompetes two years into their employment with the company and threatened to fire them if they didn't. Some employees quit, some signed, and some sued him for "unfair labor practice." The CEO lost the litigation and the noncompetes he'd had signed were then null and void. As a result, he lost most of his good employees to his competitors. His action ended up causing what he was trying to avoid in the first place. Much of this could have been avoided had he simply had his employees sign when they started, or compensated them properly when they signed later. As I said at the beginning of this section, it simply doesn't pay to be cheap with employees, or to skimp on getting good legal counsel.

Although this seems like a lot to think about, almost all of the employee handbook templates have sample language for the items I've covered. When using a template, do be sure to think about and cover any issues that might be unique to your business. Just be careful to have anything you "create" checked by your outside professionals for legality and enforceability.

Additional Resources

Sample Harassment and Anti-Discrimination Statement

It is the policy of Company X to maintain a work environment free from all forms of harassment and to insist that all employees be treated with dignity, respect, and courtesy.

1. Any actions, words, jokes, or comments based on an individual's sex, race, ethnicity, age, religion, disability, or any other legally-protected characteristic is STRICTLY PROHIBITED.

2. Any behavior toward an employee by a manager, supervisor, or co-employee which constitutes an unwelcome sexual advance or request for sexual favors—including the display of derogatory posters, cartoons, or drawings, and other verbal or physical conduct of a sexual nature—will be considered sexual harassment under this policy when:
   - Submission to such conduct is made a condition of an individual's employment.
   - Submission to or rejection of such conduct by an individual is used as the basis for employment decisions affecting such individual.
   - Such conduct has the purpose or effect of interfering with an individual's work performance or creating an offensive or intolerable work environment.

3. Any employee believing that he or she has been subjected to harassment is responsible to immediately report any such incident to his or her supervisor. If the supervisor is the cause of the problem, or if he or she seems unwilling to resolve the issue, the employee should contact the next level of management.

Every reported incident of employee harassment will be thoroughly and promptly investigated by management with the cooperation of the employee. Management shall respect the confidences and sensitivities of all personnel involved in the incident. Employees involved will be afforded protection from retaliation, and the results of any investigation of alleged harassment shall be communicated to the employee. Where charges of employee harassment are substantiated, appropriate corrective action will be taken. Appropriate action might range from counseling to termination.

HR Checklist

❑ Decide whether you need an HR head or an HR team?

❑ If you need an HR head, decide who that will be.

❑ List the specific skills and experience this person brings to the position.

❑ List the duties your HR head will handle.

❑ If you need a team, list the members and what each will handle (be sure to match skills with duties).

❑ List the outside resources are you already using.

❑ List any additional outside resources you need to add.

Fostering Collaboration Checklist

❑ Identify the departments of your company that need to be able to work together.

❑ Put a star next to any that are currently having trouble collaborating.

❑ Identify what is preventing collaboration.

❑ List their mutual goals.

❑ Decide how will you reward collaboration and achievement of goals.

❑ Make a plan for what you will do when collaboration gets off track.

Celebrating Wins Checklist

❑ List the behaviors you want to reward or recognize.

❑ List the individual accomplishments you want to recognize.

❑ List the team accomplishments you want to recognize.

❑ Describe what kinds of rewards and incentives will be valuable to your employees.

❑ Decide how you will you include families and significant others.

Company Handbook Checklist

1. Decide which resources you will use to create your employee handbook.
2. Decide who will review your handbook after it is written (be sure to choose someone who is qualified to assess it for adherence to current law, enforceability, as well as common sense).
3. Included Items Checklist:

    A. Employment Practices

       ❐ EEOC Statement

       ❐ Harassment and Anti-Discrimination Statements

       ❐ Statement of At Will status

       ❐ Attendance and Tardiness Policies

       ❐ Overtime and Work Schedule Policies

       ❐ Substance Abuse and Workplace Violence Policies

       ❐ Company Rules

       ❐ Disciplinary Process and Terminations

    B. Company Benefits
      Holidays

         ❐ Thanksgiving

         ❐ Day after Thanksgiving

         ❐ Christmas Eve

         ❐ Christmas

         ❐ New Year's Eve

         ❐ New Year's Day

         ❐ President's Day

         ❐ MLK Day

         ❐ Memorial Day

         ❐ Fourth of July

         ❐ Labor Day

Other benefits:

- ☐ Vacation
- ☐ Sick Time
- ☐ PTO
- ☐ Insurance
- ☐ Auto
- ☐ Reimbursements
- ☐ 401K/Retirement
- ☐ EAP

C. Company Property and Privacy Policies

- ☐ Internet
- ☐ Computers
- ☐ Voicemail
- ☐ Email
- ☐ Texting
- ☐ Property
- ☐ Confidentiality Statement

Recommended Reading

Catalytic Coaching: The End of the Performance Review, Gary L. Markle, Preager, 2000.

First, Break All the Rules: What the World's Greatest Managers Do Differently, Marcus Buckingham and Curt Coffman, Simon & Schuster, 1999.

1001 Ways to Reward Employees, Bob Nelson, Ph.D., Workman Publishing Company, 2005.

Please Sue Me: The Guide to Safe Hiring and Firing Practices for the Front-line Manager with a Short Attention Span, Hunter Lott, available as a download from www.hunterlott.com.

Puzzle Piece Six
Marketing

The terms "sales" and "marketing" are often used interchangeably as if there were no distinction between the two. While the two concepts are related, there are, in fact, key differences, not the least of which is timing. Marketing is everything that happens before the actual sales transaction: the ideas and processes that make someone think about buying your product or service. Sales is the art of closing the deal: matching your product or service to a need, and turning the concept of a solution into an actual solution. Those who are skilled in the art of marketing aren't necessarily good at sales; and those who have a gift for sales often aren't good at marketing. Therefore, we'll treat the two as separate pieces of the puzzle and start, in this chapter, with marketing. But remember, the two are absolutely related, and you won't be successful without both working well in tandem.

What is Marketing?

As I said above, marketing is everything else involved in the transfer of goods except the actual exchange. (Sometimes this is also called "branding.") Marketing is largely about research: determining what segment of the market you are going to own (or at least participate in), and figuring out how to properly position your product within that segment. Marketing is any activity that is involved in the "dressing" of your product or service. So let's dress up your products and services and get them ready to sell!

Pick Your Star:
What Is Your Company Really Great at Doing

This chapter is intended to give you all the elements required to create your own marketing plan. In order to do that we have to start at the beginning by answering the question: what are you the very best at? Your answer to this question will give you the blueprint for your plan. You may have many product lines and services, but I'll bet there are one or two that you do better than anyone. If you had to pick only one to focus on, which one would it be? As you think about this, consider the product or service that you are passionate about and that best represents your company's intentional purpose. If you don't really truly believe this product or service will make a difference, you'll have a very hard time marketing it convincingly.

Starting your marketing strategy this way is about picking your niche. I've seen many small companies fail to get past their first product because they wanted to be all things to all customers. The biggest barrier I see to early growth is the desire or need to take in any business that will generate immediate revenue at the cost of creating a distinctive identity. While this might seem like a good idea in the short run (money is good, right?), failing to differentiate yourself from your competitors will only hinder you in the long run. Better to choose your market space now and really work on creating that brand identity. I call this your "bright, shiny star" strategy: figure out which product is your company's "bright, shiny star," hitch your marketing wagon to that star, and ride that all the way to the bank. (The opposite of this is the "bright, shiny star syndrome," which most entrepreneurs suffer from. This happens because you are distracted by all the other bright, shiny stars and have not identified your own.

A small web development company I worked with continued to take business from customers that were not in their area of core competency. The result was frustrated clients, frustrated designers, and time lost building the core business. Once the owner started to say "no" to customers who were not identified within the target market, the company suddenly started to grow. I certainly understand how frightening it is at first to say no to business and it might sound counterintuitive, but focusing on your star area is the only way you'll achieve and sustain long-term growth.

After doing an internal evaluation, if you're still not sure which of your products or services answers the question, "What are we best at?", go to your customers. They'll tell you what you do well and what you don't.

Pick Your Market Position

When developing your marketing strategy, or branding your business, there are four generally accepted market positions you can define for yourself:

First: You were the first company to make or do this.

Only: You are the only one making or doing this.

Best: You make or deliver this product or service better than anyone else.

Most: You have the most market share for this product or service.

Let's look at each of these in more depth:

First will have the greatest impact at the start of your product or service's lifecycle. Being first to market is a strong position and you can maximize profits and position at that time. If your idea is really good, be prepared for copycats to follow quickly, which will most likely erode your price point. Although you can start out with this as your market position, you may have to move to another methodology later in the product's lifecycle. In some cases, however, "first" carries a certain amount of gravitas if messaged right. Think of Apple, where "first" defines the company as an innovator leading the way in product design.

Only is about uniqueness. You are different from anyone else. Certainly if you are the only one to provide a product or service, this becomes a strong market position to hold. The caveat is to make sure that the "only" you are marketing is something customers actually value and will therefore pay for. Also, taking the "only" position doesn't mean that your product or service has to be entirely unprecedented. If your product is similar to others but it's the only one that has a particular feature, stress that. Finally, while you can be first and only at the same time, you do need to pick which message is best for the product and your company. Which market position will have the most longevity and prestige?

Best can be a little fuzzy. By whose definition are you the best? How do you and your potential customers define "best"? Are you the highest quality? Are you the most expensive? If you choose to market your product or service as the best, you need to have a very strong message that resonates with your target audience: What does the "best" mean to them? Do they care about buying the best? Make sure your message is in alignment with your customer's needs and what they are willing to pay for, or you can be the best all the way to bankruptcy.

Most: We've all heard the saying "bigger is better." Owning the marketplace allows you a certain luxury, but be careful that you're not perceived as the bad guy because of it. Will your target audience look for the underdog because you're considered overbearing or unfair? Think about the products or services *you* buy that are positioned in this category. Does that positioning make you feel more comfortable or just frustrated? There's safety in numbers, but some consumers also value being different.

Once you've identified which of these positions you want to take, test it out on a few people. See if that market position rings true for some of your customers, employees, and investors.

The Product or Service Lifecycle

Before you go any further, it's important to know that every product or service has a lifecycle of peaks and valleys. The cycle starts in the development phase with no sales, then sales slowly ramp up to maximum popularity. The point at which your product is at peak sales is usually when competitors figure out that you're on to something. They then start to copy you and improve on what you're doing. As the product matures, sales slow down and prices drop. If you only have one product, this means the end of your company, so it's important to make sure you have multiple products or services that overlap so that you always have something at the peak of its cycle. Keep in mind that the cycle is not time based because some products and services take a long time to peak, while some stay at the top for a long time. Eventually, however, they all come down. Know this about your products and services and it won't come as a surprise when it happens. You'll already have something else waiting and ready to go.

With multiple products at different points in their lifecycle
your overall performance will remain dependable.

How To Make Money Doing What You Do Best

Now that you've decided which product or service you're really great at delivering and you've chosen your market position, how will you make money? This is where financial experts can help you create pro forma reports to help you decide if your product or service is really viable. There are many great products that never get to market because they were not financially viable. Be sure you do this evaluation *before* putting enormous amounts of time, effort, and money into research and development.

That said, remember that you don't necessarily have to make money from selling the product itself. While you market and sell a great product, you might make most of your money from service or supplies. Printer cartridges are a great example of this. Printers are essentially made to sell cartridges, which is where most of the profit is made. Maybe your after-sales services are where you'll make your money. Think about how you can differentiate those as well to make your product more attractive.

Your Unique Selling Proposition

The "Unique Selling Proposition" (USP) is a marketing theory that was first proposed by Rosser Reeves of Ted Bates and Company to explain a pattern among successful advertising campaigns of the early 1940s. The USP states that such campaigns made distinctive propositions to the customer and that this convinced them to switch brands.

These are some examples of early USPs:

- Head and Shoulders: "You get rid of dandruff."
- Domino's Pizza: "You get fresh, hot pizza delivered to your door in thirty minutes or less—or it's free."

- FedEx: "When your package absolutely, positively has to get there overnight."
- M&M's: "Melts in your mouth, not in your hand."
- Metropolitan Life: "Get Met, It Pays."
- Southwest Airlines: "We are the low-fare airline."

The psychology of advertising hasn't changed much since Reeves came up with the idea of the USP. The unique selling proposition still works, and you should have one for your company or product. Think back to the market position you selected and how you plan to make money from that, and then describe *your* unique selling proposition. Sometimes your USP will be an internal exercise, but sometimes it will become part of your advertising campaign, possibly as a tag line.

Competitive Market Analysis

Take some time to look at all your competitors and think about your product or service in relation to them. Who is out there doing what you are doing? Is the market saturated with look alikes? It's important that you always know what's happening in your market sector. Things change so rapidly that, the more information you have, the better armed you'll be to weather the ups and downs of your product's lifecycle. Being able to match the pace of the market will ensure that you are at least in the game.

Start your market analysis by listing all your competitors. Then list all the features and benefits of each company. (Remember that a feature is an attribute your product or service has, while a benefit is what your product allows your customer to do as a result. Thinking in sales terms, benefits are the remedies to your customers' pain.) Make a grid of these and see where what you offer is the same or different and where you have an advantage or disadvantage. Knowing the entire competitive landscape is key to picking the best, most marketable position for your product or service. (If it's easier to think of this in terms of a S.W.O.T. analysis, go ahead and do one for each of your competitors.)

Let's walk through an example to see what this type of analysis might look like and what it can reveal about your business. Our sample business is a large, retail sporting-goods chain that has grown rapidly. At this point in its lifecycle it's facing increasing competition from the large box stores that sell, but don't specialize in, sporting equipment. The CEO decides that they need to assess the landscape to find out how they can compete profitably. To start, they identify two axes that are unique to their business: square footage and degree of specialty (high-end) products. After plotting all their competitors on the grid, they realize they are the only one among their competitors with large stores dedicated to high-end products.

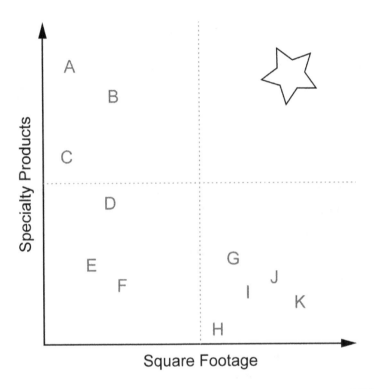

Features and Benefits Grid, Inspired by Sam Allen, Former CEO

Having gone through this process, they now have powerful information to use in truly focusing on what they do better than anyone else. As a result, they close all their smaller stores, stop buying cheaper products that are available elsewhere, and focus on their core competency. Not only do they survive in a very competitive market, they thrive.

If you were to do this exercise for your business, what would your two grid lines be? What is the space that only you occupy, or that you could occupy with a few changes? It's important that you map out this space *before* you settle on your market position so that you can maximize all your marketing resources. What a waste it would be to decide on a market position only to find out after you've launched your marketing campaign that that position is already heavily occupied.

Marketing Partners

One of the most expensive mistakes small companies make is deciding they can do their marketing all by themselves. Think back to Chapter Three: is marketing *your* core competency? Of the hundreds of CEOs I've worked with I can think of only a handful whose core competency was marketing. Even so, in each of those cases, they hired someone else to lead the effort because they were too close to the business to have perspective. So the key concept here is: *hire someone else!*

As your company grows and you bring in marketing folks to help implement your strategy, be sure to hire a firm that truly understands who you are and how to deliver your unique message. There are literally thousands of choices in the marketing world, and it can be hard to differentiate and decide which type of specialist best fits your needs.

Below is a list of some of the types of "marketing" firms you might need to hire at different points in your strategy:

- Public Relations
- Graphic Design
- Web Design
- Branding
- Marketing Strategy
- Full-Service Ad Agency
- Direct Mail
- Digital Agency
- Web Strategy
- Social Media Expert

So, where do you start? First, identify what you need. If you're a small enough business that you don't have an inside marketing department, most likely you'll need an outside firm to act as a high-level marketing director. That firm can bring in the smaller pieces as you need them after they've helped you map out an overall strategy. However you approach this, please avoid what I call the "spaghetti method" where you just try ideas and see what works. As with hiring, that is not an intentional strategy and it won't get you where you need to go. Without an intentional strategy, you'll just stay in the same place, or worse, go backwards. And, if your budget is small, don't make the mistake of buying just a piece of a marketing package. Direct mail is not a "strategy." It's much better to come up with an overall strategy that fits within that budget than to go about things piecemeal.

If you have your mission, vision, and values clearly articulated (and hopefully you do by now), you are already well on your way toward your overall marketing strategy. If you don't, you'll need to hire a firm that can take you through that process first, because your intentional purpose is the foundation that defines your approach to marketing.

When selecting a firm or person to help, look for a values fit first. Choose a company that matches your style so you'll feel comfortable working with them. Look at the work they've done: does it resonate with you? Talk to their customers to find out what the process was like. Do they specialize in working with service businesses or product businesses? Creating a brand strategy, a marketing package, or even a website is a long and intimate process, so you really want to take as much time as you need in the dating process to evaluate your potential partner. Once you've made a choice, keep in mind that marketing people are creative types. You need to strike a balance between giving them space to generate ideas, and keeping the process on track with your needs.

You may choose several people to work with, creating a team of experts to meet your specific requirements. However, keep the process transparent and ensure they have experience working this way. Some will not be comfortable with this type of arrangement as it can lessen their control, so get examples of times they have successfully worked on a team before you engage.

Keeping It Fresh

Although your brand, logos, and colors don't need to change frequently, don't hesitate to do a makeover every few years. Remember, marketing is "dressing up the baby," and who wants to wear the same clothes forever? As your company grows, you might need to refresh your talent pool as individuals can become attached to what they've created and might be reluctant to change. Toward the end of a fairly lengthy rebrand project I was involved in one of the business partners refused to switch logos. I found out later that she had created the original one and thought of herself as a marketing lead. Running up against her recalcitrance was a frustrating surprise to the whole team.

Your website, on the other hand, should be updated monthly with new information, and all the search information positioning should be refreshed even more often. The look and feel of the website should be redone every year if possible, but no less frequently than every three years at the absolute outside. Remember that, even if you're just using it as an electronic brochure, you want it to look good and be a good representation of who you are and what you do. You only have one opportunity to make a first impression. Often that will be your website. Make it a good one.

Websites and Your Total Online Presence

While we're on the topic, let's talk about websites in a little more depth. Websites are how small companies look big and compete on an international scale, and how big companies stay in touch with the real world. I cannot emphasize how much potential a well-implemented website has to gain business for you. Definitely don't do this one yourself. You'll want to partner not only with a good web designer, but with a web strategist who will take the time to understand your business and your long-term objectives. Do you want to have ecommerce capabilities? An e-newsletter? Blogs? Employee access? A secure site for customers? Employment opportunities? How important is it to be listed first when someone searches your category? A good web strategist will help you sort out your long-term web needs and how best to use your website to its maximum advantage.

Keep in mind that a website is a validation or repudiation of a company's credibility. Every sophisticated buyer or user of your product will look at your website to see who you are. Make sure your website reflects who you are. The X and Y generations do very little purchasing without first doing research on the web. A medical device service firm I worked with had a tacky website and outdated marketing materials. The CEO's Vistage group told him as much and encouraged him to hire a professional to redo everything. Taking that advice, the CEO hired a professional to give the website an overhaul. As a result the company currently has more business than it can handle. Moreover, because of opportunities created by the new website, they have branched out into a new avenue of business.

SEO Optimization

Search Engine Optimization (SEO) is vitally important for maximizing your business exposure. Essentially what it means is that when people are looking for your company, your product, or your services you'll show up at or near the top of their web search. You'll want to aim for the top three. The way to do this is to have key words on your website (as well as your blogs, e-newsletters, etc.) that include popular search terms for your business or product. For example, I'm a Leadership Coach so I want my website to come up first when someone types "leadership coach" into their search engine. In order to make sure that happens, I want to embed the term "leadership coach" many times in my site as well as in the writing I do online. You can also pay to have your business come up at the top on different search engines. A good SEO strategist will help you create a plan that is best for your company and your products or services. Remember, don't go it alone if this is not your core competency. And I'm betting it's not.

What's Your "Digital Footprint"?

We all have a "digital footprint." Just type your name into a search engine to see where you rank and what information is out there about you and your company. The key is to know that every time you make a public post or comment on the web, it will be attached to you somehow. It reminds me of what our mothers used to tell us about always wearing clean underwear in case we were in an accident. You want a clean footprint in case anyone is looking. And, if you're the CEO, they will be looking.

Business people and businesses need a good LinkedIn profile. LinkedIn is the Facebook for businesses, and has enormous potential if used correctly. You can use LinkedIn to drive business to your site, participate in discussions that get your products or services talked about, and maximize exposure for your company. You don't need to manage this yourself. Outsource it to a professional who specializes in managing web presence. That person will make sure any inappropriate content or links are removed and manage your "digital reputation."

Facebook pages are sometimes necessary for businesses, especially if you have a retail product. Facebook can be very useful to create a following for a product that is sold to consumers because consumers are Facebook's bread and butter. However, because this is primarily a social site, be careful about who you connect to, what you say, and how you use the format.

Budget

I've seen marketing budgets as much as ten percent of gross revenues and as little as .5 percent. You want to be somewhere in that range, depending on your business type and market. As part of your overall strategy, be prepared to pay for the research a good web strategy company will do for you. The payback will be worth it.

Marketing Strategy

We've touched on many of the pieces that together make up a marketing strategy. Now it's time to pull it all together. Take everything you've decided on in the last several sections and make a declaration about your strategy. It should include:

- Description of products or services
- Who will buy it
- Why they will buy it
- What your market position is (first, best, only, most)
- Your USP
- How you'll get it to market (selling strategy)
- How you'll communicate this (web, PR, print, etc.)
- What your budget is
- What your goals are
- What your timeline is
- Key Performance Indicators (see Chapter Eight for a discussion of KPIs)

Now that you know the basics of putting together a marketing strategy, what's yours?

Marketing Checklist

- ❏ Describe what your company is really great at doing.
- ❏ Describe your customers.
- ❏ Describe why those people will buy your product or service.
- ❏ Pick your market position (First, Only, Best, or Most).
- ❏ Describe how are you making money doing this.
- ❏ Describe your Unique Selling Proposition.
- ❏ Complete your competitive market analysis.
- ❏ Who are your competitors?
- ❏ List each competitor's features and benefits.
- ❏ Make a grid to see where your company fits in with the competition.
- ❏ What changes might you make based on this analysis?
- ❏ List your goals for your product or service.
- ❏ Describe how you will you get your product to market.
- ❏ List your immediate marketing needs.
- ❏ List the partners who will help you address your needs and goals.
- ❏ Decide on a realistic marketing budget and prioritize your needs and goals accordingly.
- ❏ Decide on your timeline for accomplishing your marketing goals.

Recommended Reading

Blue Ocean Strategy: How to Create Uncontested Market Space and Make Competition Irrelevant, W. Chan Kim & Renee Mauborgne, Harvard Business Review, 2005.

The Brand Called You: Make Your Business Stand Out in a Crowded Marketplace, Peter Montoya and Tim Vandehey, McGrawHill, 2008.

Competitive Advantage: Give Customers a Reason to Choose You Over Your Competitors, Jaynie Smith, Crown Business, 2006.

Duct Tape Marketing: The World's Most Practical Small Business Marketing Guide, John Jantsch, Thomas Nelson, 2008.

Puzzle Piece Seven
Sales

Now we get to the art part of the Sales and Marketing equation. You've determined what your best product or service is, picked your market position, and put together your marketing strategy. You're all ready to go out and sell your product, right? Not so fast.

Think of the sales person as the "matchmaker" between your product or service's benefits and your customers' needs. Although this person is essential to your product's success, not everyone has the personality or skills to be a great matchmaker, so let's start by describing what kinds of people make good matchmakers and what kinds of skills they need to have to make the sale.

What Makes a Great Sales Person?

Sales starts with the ability to engage someone in a conversation about their needs, and to persuade them that your product or service answers that need. Doing this without coming across as pushy is where skill tips over into art. We've all had negative sales experiences. They really stay with you, and I'll bet you could list all the things about a given bad experience that made it bad. But a really good sale often doesn't feel like a sale at all. How do those guys do that?

Really great sales executives have a natural talent for the art of conversation: they're able to gain trust quickly and really make a person feel listened to. They are outgoing, friendly, and smart. However wonderful all of these traits are, though, a sales executive must possess two key components to successfully complete a sale: the finesse to ask for the order and the capacity to follow through. I've lost count of the times I've worked with CEOs who couldn't understand why their supposedly great sales people were not selling anything. I'd ask them to define "great" in a sales person. Inevitably they would list the same things I did at the beginning of this paragraph, all of which make a person a great conversationalist, but *not* a great sales person. Without the two key components—the ask and the follow though—most sales calls will be doomed.

Hunters

Account Manager, Business Development Manager, Sales Executive: these are all titles for the person who makes contact with the customer for the purpose of closing a deal. Regardless of title or industry, people in these positions all have one thing in common: they're hunters. They love the chase (the pursuit of the deal), and they love to bring home the "prize" at the end of the hunt (the purchase order, the sale, or whatever you call it in your business). At some level, they love to win. Winning for them is not only closing this deal, but closing more deals than their peers. They are motivated by competition.

While all of that is true, the very best sales people are those who also ensure that their clients win too. Sales people are the main point of contact for the client. They know how to form lasting relationships with clients. They ensure loyalty by always making sure they deliver on whatever they said they would deliver. The best sales people take client relationships seriously because they love to grow the business and they know that sales do that. But they also know how to form relationships with their own team to make sure clients get what they need. The worst sales person is the one who is very professional to outside clients, then turns around and abuses people at the office. Good sales people are consistently authentic. And they expect to get paid for doing all that.

But let's be clear: these are rare birds. What I've just described is the *ideal* sales person. The better your sales strategy—from how you hire your sales people, to how you prepare and train them—the more likely you will come close to this ideal on your actual sales team.

Farmers

All great sales executives have a team behind them. Usually those teams consist of people called customer service representatives (or managers or assistants). These are support people, usually located in the office for the purpose of supporting the customer after a sale has been completed. This type of position is typically called a "farmer," as in someone who tends the crops once they've been planted. Being a farmer requires a different skill set from the "hunter" because this part of the customer relationship is about maintenance: making sure the customer stays happy, probing for other needs, and making sure those needs are fulfilled. Like hunters, farmers are also relationship experts. They too are outgoing, friendly, smart, great listeners, and good at follow through. What this role doesn't require is the ability to ask for the order. Temperamentally, people who gravitate to the customer service role are more risk averse and would prefer not to have their pay tied to sales performance.

You need both the hunter and the farmer in your organization. Hunters to find the deal, and farmers to tend to customers and help those relationships grow and flourish.

Phone Sales and Independent Representatives

Sometimes your sales strategy will be to sell your products over the phone. If this is the case, you still need a hunter. Even though this job is office based, it requires that all-important ability to ask for the sale. Because this job is still about the close, you need people with the skill to do that.

Depending on the size and talent pool of your company, you might choose to hire independent reps—people who sell multiple products, one of which happens to be yours—while you handle the farmer aspect within your company. Because their job is to find and close new business for you, independents need to be hunters. Keep in mind, however, because an independent's loyalty is not totally yours, handling your sales this way can be a riskier strategy.

Putting Together Your Sales Team

Once you've defined what type of hunter and farmer you need for your product or service, it's time to build the team. What kind of expertise does your product or service require? Do you need to have an outside sales force? What's the ratio of outside to inside sales people? Think about all these factors as they relate to your products.

One company I worked with had exclusive distribution through distributors and independent sales reps. The company had no sales people of their own, only internal customer-service people. They had grown the company to $10 million but couldn't seem to move past that mark. We looked at various options and decided that they needed to add at least one dedicated, internal sales person. We hired a great hunter and changed the sales structure for the reps and distributors. The result was a twenty-five percent sales increase, with both direct and channel sales growing as a result of the new strategy. After a year, the company brought on a second and third hunter with similar results.

Hiring sales people is easy. Hiring the right sales people is hard. You want to use as many profiling tools (see Chapter Four) as necessary to help you make the best hire possible. For this position you're hiring for attitude. You can train the skills. Because sales is ninety-nine percent art you want someone with natural talent that can be molded into solid skills. Remember to focus on the behaviors required for successful sales when choosing people: outgoing, people oriented, good listener, solid follow through, and competitive. Most importantly, choose people who *can* and *will* ask for the order. If they've had previous sales experience, use behavior-based interview questions to see if that experience is similar to what you're looking for. And don't forget to ask for a W-2 to prove what they say they've earned. Much as I love sales people, they do tend to be good promoters and are prone to exaggeration.

However you put together your sales team, make sure that you have the best representation for your product or service, that you're selling to your customers in a way that works for them, and that you're constantly measuring the results.

Quotas, Territories, and Compensation

Quotas

I believe quotas are always a good idea in sales. This is a group of folks who want to be measured and you absolutely want to measure your growth in sales. It's a rare win-win. Plus, your sales people are probably the easiest in your company to measure. They either sold something or they didn't. Because of their competitive nature, sales executives are always comparing themselves to the measurement, to others, or to their performance from a prior period. This is why it's very important to have appropriate quotas set in advance that both parties agree to. With reasonable, mutually agreed upon, measurable quotas, performance reviews are easy.

When I managed sales teams my process went something like this: I looked at the total sales volume from the previous year. Then I looked at the projected volume for the coming period or year. I also looked at what new products or services we were launching, as well as what new territories or initiatives we had planned for achieving our revenue goal. Then I looked at the breakdown of revenue goals from the prior year. After analyzing all that data, I sat down with my sales execs and gave them each a percentage increase I was looking for in their territory. I then invited a discussion about how that would be achieved or why it couldn't. I almost never got the response, "Oh, I can do that easily." Remember this is a negotiation because, ultimately, you want your sales people to own the number. If you just foist it on them, they'll make excuses about why it was unrealistic and never truly buy in. If you invite them into the discussion, you have a higher likelihood of achieving the goal.

After the discussion, I asked them to go away and come back when they had a written plan specifying how they would achieve the goal. Typically, a week later, I would get an outline showing me exactly which products, territories, and customers they would focus on. Occasionally they would show me how it was really impossible, or even, on rare occasions, how they could do more. The point is, by going through this exercise, it became their plan, not mine.

Territories

Territories are dependent on your products and services. Perhaps your products are better served by specialists instead of territories. But if territories make sense, take a look at whom you want to sell to and you'll quickly see how the sales territory shapes up for you. Then decide how to divide the territory among your sales team. How much geographic territory can one person handle? What travel restrictions do you have?

One caution about territories is that sales people will get complacent. They get used to orders coming in from certain clients and count on that to make their goal. This can cause them to fail to uncover all the opportunities within their territory. There are several ways to combat complacency: only give credit for the first six months of a sale; designate repeat orders as "house"; pay a smaller commission on sales to the same client after a year; or incentivize for "new" versus existing customers.

Compensation

As with measuring, paying sales people is pretty easy. First, look at what your industry pays on average for a good sales executive as well as inside customer service people. You want to pay somewhere in the mid to upper range in order to attract the very best. This is not the area to be cheap because good sales people actually pay for themselves multiple times over.

Let's say, for example, that the median pay for a good sales executive in your industry is $150,000. You probably want that package to be a sixty/forty split: sixty percent of it would be base salary and forty percent would be commission or bonus. In highly technical or long-term, enterprise-wide sales, the pay split will be less skewed towards the bonus or commission and more towards base salary; for instance, a 75/25 or even an 85/15 split. In either case, you want the base salary to be enough to live on, but not enough to be comfortable. Hunters need to be a little hungry to perform at their best.

Structuring the commission or bonus based on your goals for your sales team is key. When I had my company, we had a commission based on gross sales. My partner was frustrated that our margin kept eroding even as sales were growing. So I changed the sales commission to pay only on margin, and, surprise, our margin percentage and sales went up dramatically. Whatever you want your sales people to do—to sell or to grow or both— tie it to the commission or bonus portion of their compensation. You'll be glad you did.

Additional bonuses or incentives are always a good way to jump-start a new product launch, or get rid of old inventory. Sales people will go where the money is because they tend to have a "what's in it for me" mentality, and will do what it takes to maximize their share. That's not a bad thing. It's how sales people are wired and it can be very, very good for your company.

Before laying out your compensation structure, be sure to research the standards in your industry. You might be in an industry that is straight commission; for example, real estate, brokerage, car sales, and insurance. Typically commissions are high in these industries because you have no costs unless the deal is closed. It takes a certain breed of hunter who is very confident to work for straight commission. They are usually very independent and enjoy risk, so don't think you'll be able to monitor or track their activities too closely.

Scripts

I know some people who say that scripts are overrated and a good sales person just knows what to say. That's not exactly true. A good sales person knows *how* to approach people and engage in conversation, but you have to define *what* they say about your product. And no one is particularly good at articulating those details at first. It takes some practice.

Think about your vision and values. With those as the basis for your scripts, your pitch package should include all of the following components: an "elevator speech," a phone script, a gatekeeper script, and an in-person presentation.

Elevator Speech

Your elevator speech is a short description of what you do with the goal of starting a conversation. Think of it this way: you step onto an elevator, you punch the button for the next floor, and just as the doors close, the person next to you asks you what you do. You have just until the next floor to explain, so by necessity your speech has to be concise and to the point. When I was a chair for Vistage International, my elevator speech was: "I run groups of CEOs who help each other with their businesses." The point is to grab people's attention so they ask a question. If they do that, you know your elevator speech is successful because you've started a conversation. In my case, people would always say, "Really, how do you do that?"

In this case, you'll be writing an elevator speech for your product or service. My good friend Lorraine Howell is an expert in this field and has worked with thousands of people helping them perfect their elevator speeches. I highly recommend her book, *Give Your Elevator Speech a Lift,* either to help you get started or to fine tune the speech you already have. Once you have yours down, make sure everyone at the company knows it. They're your free billboards. Don't waste that advertising opportunity!

Phone Script

I can't emphasize enough how important it is for anyone doing cold calls, follow up, customer service calls, or any repetitive outward-facing client calls to initially follow a script until they can do those calls in their sleep.

This does not mean those people should read from a script as if they're automatons; rather, it means memorizing the ideas and then saying those in their own style to make the communication authentic and genuine. The reason for the script is so that you manage the message. These people are touching your customers: it's imperative that the message be accurate, intentional, and aligned with your values.

Start by deciding what the goal or purpose of a given call is. If it is to ascertain interest in a particular product, start with some introductory questions. Some can be closed questions (these require only a yes or no answer), and some can be open ended. The script should include a matrix of follow up choices depending on the customer's answer. In other words, if the customer answers "yes" to a question, there is one series of follow up questions; if the customer answers "no," then the script goes in a different direction. All potential answers should be accounted for so that the sales person knows exactly what to say and always sounds professional.

Salespeople should have their scripts in front of them at all times, following along while maintaining a conversational tone. The goal of the call should be at the forefront at all times. You can even put it at the top of the script.

At the end, the salesperson should thank the customer or prospect and close with the appropriate followup item. (See the sample scripts at the end of this chapter.)

Gatekeeper Script

A gatekeeper script adheres to all the same rules as the phone script, but its purpose is different. The purpose of the Gatekeeper Script is get to the decision maker. These days anyone can find out who they should be talking to by doing a review of a company's website. Once that homework is complete, your salespeople can begin calling. At that point they'll likely run into a "gatekeeper," the person responsible for protecting the decision maker's time. You won't get far by being belligerent to the gatekeeper. Instead your script should include polite questions with the goal of turning the gatekeeper into your ally. As with the phone script, always remember what the goal is: to get information to your target, to speak with your target, or to make an appointment. (See the sample script at the end of this chapter.)

The In-Person Presentation

Your strategy for an in-person presentation will depend on multiple factors:

- What is the product or service?
- Who is your audience?
- How much time do you have?
- What is your goal for the appointment?

The most important thing to remember here is that you have a finite amount of time to get your message across. Time is so valuable these days that, if you don't connect with the individual on the things that are important to them in the first ten minutes, you'll lose them. If yours is a highly personal product or service, forget PowerPoint and focus on the conversation and leave behind a brochure highlighting product features and benefits. If it's a very technical product, make sure you know what the customer's pain points are ahead of time so you can speak directly to those.

Perhaps you're on a fact-finding mission to explore whether there is even a fit for the features and benefits of your product. If that is the case, start asking questions and let the customer talk. Information gathering is better done in small groups or one-on-one meetings so the sales executive has time to build rapport. Once all the data is gathered, then a formal presentation that addresses all the needs of the customer can be made with PowerPoint or notebooks or whatever medium best conveys the solution to their problem. Whatever the goal, however, the key to the in-person presentation is that the salesperson should do the least amount of talking but the most questioning.

How you approach the presentation depends on all of the above factors, starting with the four questions. Once you know the answers, you can put together a sales presentation and tailor it as needed to the individual customer. However, there are a couple of critical factors that cannot be overlooked, though they frequently are. First, preparation is essential to a successful meeting or presentation. You cannot wing it because you won't get a second chance if you fail. You may be green, but that's no excuse for not preparing. Second, never leave without clearly deciding on a next step. The next step might be:

- A quote or proposal to be given by a certain date
- A follow up call
- More data will be provided
- A reference needs to be called
- There is no next step because this is not the right fit

Whatever the desired outcome of the in-person call, know it ahead of time. You don't know if you've won if you don't know where the goal posts are. I always encourage sales professionals to do a plus/delta on each call, either at the end of the call or the end of the day. What went well? What could I have done better? With each call you gain knowledge, experience, and confidence. Make sure the whole team is leveraging that.

Objections

Handling objections is a huge part of the art of selling. Rarely will you find yourself pitching to someone who just pulls out their wallet and pays for your product without some sort of objection. The more expensive the item, the more objections you're likely encounter. Learning to deal with these effectively is essential to sales success.

For each product or service, there are at least six common objections. Objections often take the form of questions, but make no mistake about what they are. The nature of the objection will tell you something about your customers and how to respond without making them feel foolish about their concerns.

- **Price:** When customers say an item is too expensive, they're really saying you haven't given them enough detail so they can appreciate the value of your product or service. Rarely does someone tell you your product is too cheap.
- **Information:** Asking for more data tells you this person is probably an analytical, so you'll need to know your facts or bring along a specialist to cover the details.
- **Nonresponsive:** When a customer doesn't respond to you, it usually means you haven't asked enough needs-based questions to uncover that person's real need.
- **Talk:** Someone who talks but doesn't ask many questions about the product is usually just a people person. You're going to have to get to business at some point so you'll need to take more control of the conversation. Sometimes talk is just a way to divert your attention from the fact that this person: a.) doesn't want your product, or b.) doesn't have the authority to buy your product. Don't waste your time or theirs if there isn't a mutual fit.
- **Options:** Someone who wants all possible configurations is a person who likes options. Respond by giving them choices.
- **Bluntness:** Someone who is very blunt and just wants the facts has little time to waste on chitchat. Get to the point and get out.

Once you've developed answers for the most common objections for your product or service, keep them updated as technology, products, and times change. Always be the most knowledgeable person about your products. Know what people are saying about it, both good and bad, and know how to respond to that. When confronted with a new objection that you can't answer, admit you don't know, but promise the customer you'll find out and get back to them. Take that back to the office for discussion. After you've followed up with the customer, add that objection and answer to your list. Customers will forgive you for not knowing something once, but they won't do it again.

Training

Continuous training is mandatory for anyone in sales. Products, processes, technology, and people change so quickly that, in order to be good at what you do, you need to constantly ask, "What don't I know?"

A sales executive who doesn't embrace continuous training or learning will soon become a dinosaur, so be sure to encourage and provide ongoing training to make sure that doesn't happen in your company. The following are just a few of the basic training subjects for any sales team:

- Buying styles
- Product training
- Personality types
- Sales methodology
- Presentation training
- Elevator pitch training
- Prospecting
- Handling objections

Depending on your specific training needs, you can set both tone and expectations for training by setting up a schedule a year in advance and arranging for trainers or experts to come in and speak on different topics. I don't have an opinion as to whether or not training should be mandatory, but I would make certain judgments about those who don't attend training, and I would watch their numbers closely. If they're not making quota, I'd make training mandatory until they get back on track.

Whatever the training topics or schedule, be sure to take the following factors into account when deciding on the program:

- What are the vision and values of your organization?
- What are you trying to accomplish this year?
- What were your biggest sales failures and successes last year and why?
- What is the one sales problem that, if solved, would have the biggest ROI on your bottom line?
- Is your sales process being followed?
- Is your organization true to your sales strategy?
- Who else in the organization should join in training?

Some other points to consider about training:

- Not everyone learns at the same pace or has the same style, so provide different modes for learning: classroom, online, books, seminars, etc. Have your best people teach subjects or strategies they excel at.
- Have a continuous schedule of training so you can continue to grow and include more people. Find different ways to internally advertise trainings. People will need to hear it multiple ways and more than once for the message to get across.
- As with so many of the other pieces of the puzzle, let your company values guide you on training. If one of the values of your company is "innovation," make your trainings innovative. If one of your values is fun, then you'd better have some fun with training.
- And always have a way to measure if training is working. Sales results will tell you a little, but employee satisfaction might tell you more.

Sales Process

Now that you've had time to think about the structure of your sales team and how you're going to sell, it's time to map out the process. From the first touch point—your product—what are all the steps you'll need to take to get to the end point, the sale?

With a more complicated or technical product the process might look like this: the first step is your inside team making a cold call. That gets an appointment for the outside rep, and the outside rep makes a visit with a potential customer. The outside rep assesses the customer's need and generates a quote. Then someone follows up with the customer and takes an order. The order is fulfilled and installed. Then a service team reaches out to set up ongoing maintenance. In a year, the same team contacts the customer to talk about an upgrade. If your product is not complex, the process will probably also be simpler, but the basic idea is still the same.

What you are doing in mapping out your sales process is thinking through the lifecycle of your products and services as they relate to the customer or end user. It's critical that you know all of these points before you start selling, and that your sales people know too. Most importantly, your process needs to be better than your competitor's. You need to know your product, your market, and your target customer better. Knowledge is power, especially in sales.

Pricing Strategy

My eyes were really opened to the power of price increases and discounts—and especially how they affect the bottom line—when I was first introduced to the Price Increase Table (courtesy of RealTime CEO) which shows how much dollar volume you can lose (drop in sales) while maintaining the same dollars of gross profit after a price increase. For example, if you have a twenty-five percent gross margin and you raise a price by five percent, you can have a 16.67 percent drop in sales volume and still make the same gross profit. And gross profit is the more important number because that is what keeps the lights on. Understanding this should give you some courage to make reasonable and regular increases in order to keep your business growing.

Now that you know you *can* raise your prices, how should you do it? I was always told that a business needs to raise prices at least once a year in order to stay ahead of pricing increases from suppliers and vendors. Doing this also sets a precedent for your customers, and gives both of you some leverage when negotiating.

I once worked with a company that had not raised prices in seven years. They were hemorrhaging cash when I finally convinced them they had to raise prices or go out of business. They made a modest price increase—five to ten percent by product—and, not only did most of their customers stay, many of them said they had wondered when prices were going to go up. The company lost about five percent of their sales volume, but they more than made up for it in better margins.

That said, raising prices every year, just because you can, is also not a good strategy. When looking at your pricing, you need to examine several factors:

- Where are we on the pricing scale compared to our competitors?
- What are our competitors doing in terms of price increases?
- Have our operating costs gone up?
- Are we at or near the maximum amount people will pay for this product or service?

Price Increase Table

(% drop in Sales that can be sustained to maintain the same $ Gross Profit after price increase.)

Price Increase	\ Gross Margin → 10%	15%	20%	25%	30%	35%	40%	45%	50%	55%	60%
2%	16.67%	11.76%	9.09%	7.41%	6.25%	5.41%	4.76%	4.26%	3.85%	3.51%	3.23%
3%	23.08%	16.67%	13.04%	10.71%	9.09%	7.89%	6.98%	6.25%	5.66%	5.17%	4.76%
4%	28.57%	21.05%	16.67%	13.79%	11.76%	10.26%	9.09%	8.16%	7.41%	6.78%	6.25%
5%	33.33%	25.00%	20.00%	16.67%	14.29%	12.50%	11.11%	10.00%	9.09%	8.33%	7.69%
10%	50.00%	40.00%	33.33%	28.57%	25.00%	22.22%	20.00%	18.18%	16.67%	15.38%	14.29%
15%	60.00%	50.00%	42.86%	37.50%	33.33%	30.00%	27.27%	25.00%	23.08%	21.43%	20.00%
20%	66.67%	57.14%	50.00%	44.44%	40.00%	36.36%	33.33%	30.77%	28.57%	26.67%	25.00%
25%	71.43%	62.50%	55.56%	50.00%	45.45%	41.67%	38.46%	38.71%	33.33%	31.25%	29.41%
30%	75.00%	66.67%	60.00%	54.55%	50.00%	46.15%	42.86%	40.00%	37.50%	35.29%	33.33%

Price Discount Table

(% increase in Sales needed to maintain the same $ Gross Profit after a discount.)

Price Discount	\ Gross Margin → 10%	15%	20%	25%	30%	35%	40%	45%	50%	55%	60%
2%	25.00%	15.38%	11.11%	8.70%	7.14%	6.06%	5.26%	4.65%	3.85%	3.77%	3.45%
3%	42.86%	25.00%	17.65%	13.64%	11.11%	9.38%	8.11%	7.14%	5.66%	5.77%	5.26%
4%	66.67%	36.36%	25.00%	19.05%	15.38%	13.90%	11.11%	9.76%	7.41%	7.84%	7.14%
5%	100.00%	50.00%	33.33%	25.00%	20.00%	16.67%	14.29%	12.50%	9.09%	10.00%	9.09%
10%	NA	200.00%	100.00%	66.67%	50.00%	40.00%	33.33%	28.57%	16.67%	22.22%	20.00%
15%	NA	NA	300.00%	150.00%	100.00%	75.00%	60.00%	50.00%	23.08%	37.50%	33.33%
20%	NA	NA	NA	400.00%	200.00%	133.33%	100.00%	80.00%	28.57%	57.14%	50.00%
25%	NA	NA	NA	NA	500.00%	250.00%	166.67%	125.00%	33.33%	83.33%	71.43%
30%	NA	NA	NA	NA	NA	600.00%	300.00%	200.00%	37.50%	120.00%	100.00%

The Power of Prices

Courtesy of Nick Setchell, Founder RealTime CEO

- How many customers will go away due to the price increase? (Use the table to determine impact on your margins.)

Once you've determined the answers to these questions, you can decide on a schedule for regular price increases (whether that's annually, every eighteen months, every two years, or only as costs rise). People don't like surprises, so let your customers know in advance what your strategy is for price increases and what sort of advance notice you'll give them. Then, if you decide not to raise prices one year, your customers feel like you've given them a gift. You win on that one!

The Price Discount Table shows the opposite of the Price Increase Table. It shows you the percent increase in sales needed to maintain the same dollars in Gross Profit after a discount. Let's say you have a twenty-five percent Gross Margin and you decide to give a five percent discount on the product or service. You'll need to increase your sales volume by at least twenty-five percent just to stay even. So, before you decide on any discounting, check the table to make sure you aren't dipping into gross margin too much in case your sales volume doesn't rise.

Customer Ranking

Probably eighty percent of your revenue is coming from twenty percent of your customers. Part of any good sales strategy is to know who your good customers are and why. You already have lots of good information on your existing customers. Start using it to inform your sales strategy.

Let's do a fun little exercise and determine what makes a good customer. Take a big whiteboard and jot down everything that makes a good customer for your company. Include things like type of work, volume, pay practices, etc. Your list should have about five to ten items on it. Now look at that list and decide how many items would have to be a "yes" for you to give a customer an A grade. Some of these items might be nonnegotiable in order to earn an A. Now decide how many for a B or a C. (If you prefer, you can also score these on a numerical scale.) Now list all of your customers and grade each one according to your scale. If a customer doesn't earn even a C grade, it's time to reevaluate your relationship or your strategy. Do this on an annual basis to decide which of your customers you should be paying more or less attention to or firing! (See the list at the end of this chapter for some ideas for customer criteria.)

I recently did this with the small medical device company I mentioned in the last chapter and we came up with a list of seven items that make a good customer, two of which were nonnegotiable. An A had to have seventy-five percent of the items as a "yes" including both nonnegotiables. A B had to have fifty percent, with a C assigned for anything less than fifty percent.

After making the list and setting the criteria, the company rated its customers. It was amazing for some of the managers to find out that customers they'd always thought of as good, didn't in fact grade very well because they always paid their bill late or were short. The owner was surprised to hear what the technicians in the field thought of customers based on how they were treated or integrated into the client's site.

Rank all your clients. What interesting things show up for you? What will you do differently as a result? Now, rather than working so hard on your C customers, which are almost always the ones who want to buy on price and price only, you can focus on you're A and B customers. What can you do to keep your A customers happy and what can you do to make your B customers into A customers? All the research will tell you that it's almost ten times easier to keep and grow a client than it is to find a new one. Make sure you're putting your energy into your top customers!

Bringing It All Together

Over the course of this chapter, you've learned how to put together a sales strategy that addresses the following questions:

- Who are we selling to?
- What does our ideal customer look like (base this on your rankings)?
- Who will sell our product or service (inside, outside, independent reps)?
- How are they compensated?
- What is our territorial strategy (national, regional, international)?
- What is our sales structure/What does the team look like?
- How will we sell our product or service (in person, phone, retail, e-commerce, etc.)?
- What tools will we use (scripts)?
- What is our sales process?

- What is our pricing strategy?
- What training will we provide?
- What are our sales goals?

Now that you've read the last two chapters, spend some time reflecting on your overall Marketing and Sales Strategy because they're critical to the success of your products and your company. Great products fail not because they're not great. They fail because they're not presented so that people view them as the solution to their problem, and therefore they don't sell. Lots of terrible products sell very well because the package creates a false need. If marketing is a science and sales is an art, you need both to succeed.

Additional Resources

Sample Call Scripts

Purpose: To get an appointment with the Decision Maker

Call 1

Salesperson:	Hello, my name is John with the XYZ company, and I'd like to see if you have a few minutes to meet with me to learn about how we might help you help your clients.
Target:	No, send me some information.
Salesperson:	Certainly, I'm happy to do so. I have your address as XX, is that correct?
Target:	Yes.
Salesperson:	Great, I'll send you some information and next time I'm in the area, I'll stop by and see if you have a minute to meet with me in person. Thank you for your time.

Call 2

Salesperson:	Hello, my name is Jane with the XYZ company, and I'd like to see if you have a few minutes to meet with me to learn how we might help you help your clients.
Target:	Who are you?
Salesperson:	I'm Jane with the XYZ company, and we help people stay in their homes as long as possible. Is that something your clients are interested in?
Target:	Yes.
Salesperson:	Great, I could come by on Friday or Tuesday. Will you be in the office either of those days? I promise not to take more than five minutes.
Target:	Sure, Friday would be good.
Salesperson:	Great, thank you, I'll see you at ten o'clock on Friday.

Call 3

Salesperson: Hello, my name is John with the XYZ company, and I'd like to see if you have a few minutes to meet with me to learn how we might help you help your clients.

Target: No.

Salesperson: Okay, I thought it was important for some of your clients to stay in their homes as they age?

Target: It is.

Salesperson: Okay, may I send you some information on our company, or direct you to our website? We really do make it easy for people to age in their own homes.

Target: Sure, go ahead and send me something.

Salesperson: Great, thank you, I'll put that in the mail today and drop by next time I'm in the neighborhood.

Gate Keeper Script

Salesperson: Hello, my name is John with the XYZ company, and I'd like to see if Mr. Smith has a few minutes to meet with me to learn about how we might help you help your clients.

Target: I'm sorry, he doesn't allow meetings with people he doesn't know.

Salesperson: Okay, I can certainly understand that and I don't want to be a pest, so how would I best go about introducing myself to him?

Target: You can send me something and I'll see if he wants to meet with you.

Salesperson: Oh, great, thank you so much for your help. What's your name?

Target: Sarah.

Salesperson: Thanks Sarah, I'll go ahead and send it to your attention, and then follow up with you next week to make sure you've received it. Will that work for you?

Target: Sure, thank you.

Salesperson: Thanks again for your time, and I appreciate your help Sarah!

Sample Customer Ranking Criteria

- Prompt payment history
- Using more than one product
- Good communication habits
- Location
- Key contact
- Values match
- Strategic partner
- Buying history
- Return history
- Client volume
- Payment history
- Types of products
- Geography
- Technical help needed
- Referrals given
- Easy to deal with
- Profitability

Sales Strategy Checklist

- ❏ Describe your customers.
- ❏ Describe how you sell your product or service (in person, on the phone, retail, e-commerce, etc.).
- ❏ List any changes you need to make in how you sell your product or service.
- ❏ Describe who sells your product or service (inside, outside, independent reps.).
- ❏ List any changes you need to make in who sells your product or service.
- ❏ Describe how your sales people are compensated.
- ❏ List any changes you need to make to how your salespeople are compensated.
- ❏ Describe your sales structure.
- ❏ Describe/list your sales team.
- ❏ List any changes you need to make to your sales structure or sales team.
- ❏ Describe your territorial strategy (national, regional, international).
- ❏ Develop the following sales tools:
    - ❏ Elevator pitch
    - ❏ Phone script
    - ❏ Gatekeeper phone script
    - ❏ Standard objections and response
    - ❏ In person sales presentation
- ❏ List trainings you are currently providing to keep your sales team sharp.
- ❏ List any trainings you need/would like to add.
- ❏ Describe your sales goals.

☐ Describe/develop your sales process.

Pricing Strategy Checklist

☐ Identify where you are on the pricing scale compared to your competitors.

☐ Are your competitors raising prices? How often? How much?

☐ Are you at or near the maximum amount people will pay for this product or service?

☐ How many of your customers will go away if you increase your prices?

☐ Have your operating costs gone up?

☐ Decide how often you will increase prices and by how much.

☐ Decide how you will keep your customers informed in advance about price increases.

Customer Ranking Checklist

☐ Describe five to ten qualities that define a good customer for your company.

☐ Identify which of these a customer must have to earn an A grade (put a star next to nonnegotiables).

☐ Identify which of these a customer must have to earn a B.

☐ Identify which of these a customer must have to earn a C.

☐ List your customers and grade them.

☐ Identify what you can do to keep your A customers happy.

☐ Identify what you can do to turn your B customers into A customers.

Recommended Reading

Give Your Elevator Speech a Lift: How to Craft Your Own 30-Second Commercial, Lorraine Howell, Book Publisher's Network, 2010.

How to Win Friends and Influence People, Dale Carnegie, Simon & Schuster, 2009.

Neuromarketing: Understanding the Buy Buttons in Your Customer's Brain, Patrick Renvoise and Christophe Morin, Thomas Nelson, 2007.

Selling the Invisible: A Field Guide to Modern Marketing, Harry Beckwith, Business Plus, 2012.

Selling to VITO the Very Important Top Officer: Get to the Top. Get to the Point. Get to the Sale, Anthony Parinello, Adams Media, 2010.

Puzzle Piece Eight
Financial Metrics

Every company needs a scorecard. Without one, you're flying with a blindfold on and you're more likely to crash than you are to succeed. Nonetheless, it's not uncommon for businesses to operate without good financial measuring tools in place. This happens in part because we all come to our businesses with our own personal beliefs about money. These beliefs (derived from our life experiences, including our family and education) color our understanding of money—who should have it and what should be done with it by those who do have it. But it also happens because many of us don't have a basic business finance education. Without this type of education, you might not have the basic tools you need to successfully run your business. Not having these tools makes it hard to grow your business intentionally over the long-term, while also making you more susceptible to fraud.

However averse you may be to number crunching, basic business finances are something you have to learn. Even if you've learned how to read a Profit and Loss Statement and a Balance Sheet in the course of running your business, you probably don't know as much as you think you do. After I bought my own company, I took a three-day course in business finances at what was then Seafirst Bank. Boy, did that open my eyes to everything I didn't know about my own company's finances. By the end of the three days, though, I had gained a basic vocabulary of finance and was at least able to ask the right questions of the right people. Similarly, you don't have to become a finance professional. You just need to know enough of the basics to really see how your company operates. When you can do that, you can run your business intentionally to weather ups and downs and ultimately achieve your overall goals.

Basic Financial Terms

In order to begin to have a basic understanding of business finances, you have to start with terminology. Below is a list of some of the most common financial terms (and the tools they describe) that you and your executive team should understand. This list is not exhaustive, but it should give you a good start. You can always dig deeper in one of the books listed at the end of this chapter.

AP Accounts Payable.

AR Accounts Receivable.

Accrual Basis Accrual basis accounting records income items when they are earned (rather than when payment is received), and records deductions when expenses are incurred (rather than when payment is made).

Asset A resource with monetary value, including cash, accounts receivable, inventory, real estate, machinery, collectibles, and securities.

Balance Sheet A business's financial statement that provides a picture of its assets, debts, and net worth at a specific time.

COGS Cost of Goods Sold.

Cash Basis Cash basis accounting records revenue when cash is received and records expenses when cash is paid.

Current Assets Assets that can be converted to cash within a year.

Current Liabilities Liabilities that must be paid within a year.

EBITDA Earnings Before Income, Taxes, Depreciation, and Amortization.

Fixed Assets Any long-term asset (such as a building, tract of land, or patent) that will not be converted to cash within a year.

Gross Margin Amount after cost of goods are taken from revenue.

Income Statement (also called a Profit and Loss Statement) The financial statement that presents both revenues and expenses during a specified time period.

Liabilities The claims of those who have made loans to a company; debts.

Liquidity The ability or ease with which assets can be converted into cash; also the degree to which one can obtain the full cash value of an investment.

Net Income Profit after taxes.

Net Profit A company's profitability after all costs have been accounted for. Also called "the bottom line."

Net Profit Margin A measure of a company's profitability and efficiency, calculated by dividing Net Profit by sales.

Net Sales Amount of sales found by subtracting customer returns, discounts, and allowances from money collected for goods and services.

Net Worth Value found by subtracting all liabilities from all assets.

Operating Costs and Expenses The costs and expenses necessary to operate a company; this includes manufacturing, marketing, research and development, and operating costs.

Operating Income The income derived after subtracting operating costs and expenses from net sales.

Operating Margin A measure of a company's profitability and efficiency, calculated by dividing operating profit by sales.

Operating Profit The profit earned from a company's core operations only, not including any profit from investments. (Sales – Operating Expenses including production costs = Operating Profit)

Profit Margin The margin found by dividing a company's post-tax net earnings by sales. Profit margin measures how well one company can earn money from sales relative to others.

Return On Equity (ROE) The value found by dividing the company's net income by its net assets. ROE measures the amount a company earns on shareholder investments.

Total Assets The sum found by adding property, plant, and equipment asset values to current asset values.

Total Debt to Total Assets The ratio found by dividing short- and long-term debts by the total assets of the firm. This ratio measures a company's financial risk, showing how much of the business's property has been financed by debt.

Total Liabilities The liabilities found by adding current liabilities to long-term debts.

Key Financial Indicators

Following are the Key Financial Indicators every business should be tracking, regardless of industry. They measure the financial health of the company and act as signposts by which you can make the best decisions for your business. It's not important for you to memorize the formulas. It is important that you know what they mean and that your financial person—Bookkeeper, Controller, CFO, or outside Accountant—provide the data for those indicators on a regular basis so that you can measure them over time. The key is to plan and course correct as needed based on your signposts.

Following these indicators is, of course, in addition to your standard financial statements (Profit and Loss/Income, Balance Sheet, and Cash Flow). You should receive these statements by the fifth to seventh working day of each month. If your accounting person can't provide you these on this schedule, find one who can.

Balance Sheet Ratios

Your balance sheet gives a snapshot of your business's overall health as of the date on which it was calculated, and for that date only. It describes the assets, liabilities, and ownership position as of that date. In order to use it to understand the health of the business, you need to compare it over several time periods. The reason these ratios are important is because they measure the amount of risk in your business. Also known as Liquidity Ratios, these measure your company's ability to survive a short-term financial crisis. When revenues continue to climb while the following ratios decline—a scenario that happens frequently in fast growth companies—lack of cash will not allow you to finance the growth.

Current Ratio measures whether you have enough current assets (defined as anything that can be changed to cash within a year's period) to meet your current liabilities.

Current Ratio = Current Assets ÷ Current Liabilities

Debt to Equity Ratio measures how much your company is financed by borrowing as compared to owner equity. This ratio plays a major role in determining how much you can borrow and at what interest rate. If you have bank financing, this is the ratio the bankers will watch.

Debt to Equity Ratio = Total Liabilities ÷ Net Worth

Quick Ratio measures your company's ability to use its current cash or assets to pay current liabilities. Quick assets include those that can be converted to cash at or near their book value.

Quick Ratio = Cash + Marketable Securities + AR

Leverage Ratio measures your business's capacity to incur debt as a multiple of EBITDA. A conservative ratio would be less than two.

Leverage Ratio = Debt ÷ EBITDA

Profit and Loss (P&L) Ratios

The P&L statement focuses on revenues, expenses, and net income (or loss) over a defined period of time. It measures your company's ability to turn revenue into profit.

Gross Profit or Gross Margin measures how much money you have left after subtracting the COGS, including direct sales expenses (these are usually referred to as "above the line" expenses.) If you sell a product for a dollar and it costs eighty cents to build or buy it, your gross profit is twenty cents. This twenty cents has to cover all your other expenses.

Gross Profit = Revenue – Cost of Goods Sold

Net Operating Profit and EBITDA represent how much money you have left after operating expenses have been paid. This is also referred to as your "net." (Operating expenses and net profit are considered "below the line.") Net Operating Profit should not be confused with cash, because it doesn't mean you still have it in hand. You simply earned it. People often confuse EBITDA (Earnings Before Interest, Taxes, Depreciation, and Amortization) and Net Operating Profit, but actually they're not quite the same. You may also have heard of this simply as EBIT, without depreciation and amortization. Depending on which software your financial person is using, interest, taxes, depreciation, and amortization might be mixed in with Operating Expenses. If someone asks for any of these three (Net Profit, EBITDA or EBIT), be sure to remember that they are slightly different. You'll want to know all three calculations for your business.

Net Operating Profit = Gross Profit – Operating Expenses*
*This is sometimes referred to as Selling (indirect), General, and Administrative (SG&A).

Net Profit Net Profit is what's left after *all* other expenses, including depreciation, amortization, interest, and taxes.

Net Profit =
Net Operating Profit – Interest –Other Expenses – Taxes

Operating Ratios

Operating ratios combine information from the balance sheet and the income statement to provide more detailed information about what's really happening with your business.

Gross Margin Although this is sometimes used synonymously with Gross Profit, it's actually an offshoot. Gross Margin measures the percentage of every dollar of sales that becomes gross profit. For example, a Gross Margin of fifty percent means that you earn fifty cents of Gross Profit for every dollar in sales.

Gross Margin = Gross Profit ÷ Sales

Pre-Tax Profit Margin Similar to Gross Margin, your PreTax Profit Margin is the percentage of profit for every dollar of sales. You would use this to compare your results with those of others in your industry.

Pretax Profit Margin = Pretax Profit ÷ Sales

Sales to Assets Ratio measures the amount of sales generated for every dollar of assets owned by your business. For example, a Sales to Assets Ratio of 3.5 means that you generate $3.50 in sales for every dollar of your assets.

Sales to Asset Ratio = Sales ÷ Total Assets

Return on Assets Ratio is similar to Sales to Assets Ratio, but measures instead how much *profit* you generate for every dollar of assets.

Return on Assets Ratio = Pretax Profit ÷ Total Assets

Return on Equity Ratio tells owners how well their investment in their business is doing. Even though it's hard for entrepreneurs to look at their businesses as investments, they really should. The bank certainly does, as do potential buyers.

Return on Equity Ratio = Pretax Profit ÷ Equity

Inventory Turnover Ratio measures how many times a year you sell your inventory. There are two ways to calculate this ratio: either using sales cost or using selling price. Although it's more typical to use actual cost rather than selling price, either one will work for the calculation. Just make sure you use comparable numbers for the dividend and the divisor. In other words, if you use sales cost, you must also use inventory cost. Conversely, if you use selling price, you must also use inventory selling price.

Inventory Turnover Ratio =
Cost of Goods Sold (COGS) ÷ Average Inventory

Days in Inventory Ratio measures how long, on average, it takes to turn over your inventory.

Days in Inventory Ratio =
Days in Inventory Period ÷ Inventory Turnover

Accounts Receivable Turnover Ratio tracks how many times per year you collect your Accounts Receivable.

AR Turnover Ratio = Sales ÷ Accounts Receivable

Collections Period Ratio (Days Outstanding) measures how often, on average, you collect your accounts receivable. This is also called "days to collect," and is an important measure to track, especially if cash flow is an issue. The sooner you collect your AR, the sooner you have cash!

Collections Period Ratio = 365 ÷ AR Turnover

Accounts Payable Turnover Ratio Similar to the receivables side, this measures how many times a year you pay your Accounts Payable.

AP Turnover Ratio = 365 ÷ AP

Payable Period Ratio measures how often you pay your accounts payable.

Payable Period Ratio = 365 ÷ AP Turnover Ratio

Sustainable Growth Rate

Your Sustainable Growth Rate is the rate at which your business can grow and not run out of cash. This calculation will show you how much revenue increase you can absorb without increasing your Debt to Equity Ratio. The higher your Debt to Equity Ratio, the higher the risk in your business. You'll have to decide for yourself your level of risk tolerance. If you're using bank financing, you'll also have to find out your bank's requirements.

However, the Sustainable Growth Rate should not be confused with the rate you *can* grow. You can grow much faster, but growth comes with risk if you don't also grow your profits and manage your assets. If you have a low level of debt, depending on the opportunities available, you can leverage financing to grow at a faster rate. Therefore, the sustainable growth rate can be calculated one of two ways: either assuming no new debt (Scenario A), or assuming a new level of debt (Scenario B).

Same Debt-To-Equity Ratio

FORMULA	$$\frac{(\text{Net Profit\%}) \times (1+\text{Debt/Equity})}{(\text{Var. Assets \% to Sales}) - [\text{NPM\%} \times (1 + \text{Debt}^*/\text{Equity})]}$$ $^*\text{Debt} = \text{Total Liabilities}$

	Scenario A	Scenario B
A) Net Margin % =	_____	_____
B) Debt =	_____	_____
C) Equity =	_____	_____
D) Assets to Sales % =	_____	_____

CALCULATION

$$\frac{A \times (1 + B/C)}{D - [A \times (1 + B/C)]}$$

	Scenario A	Scenario B
1) B/C =	_____	_____
2) +1 =	_____	_____
3) x A =	_____	_____
4) D - Step 3 =	_____	_____
5) Step 3 / Step 4 =	_____	_____

The final percentage is the sustainable growth rate, which is important because every business should know how fast it can grow without outside funding. You really need to take some time to understand this fundamental indicator because, without it, your plans for growth are likely to be unreasonable or unrealistic.

Break-Even Analysis

Your break-even number is the amount of sales that creates just enough revenue to cover all your expenses without a loss *or* a profit. Knowing your break even is critical to understanding what decisions you can make in your business and when. This is often called your "nut," or knowing what it takes to cover expenses. Everything above the nut is extra. On the other hand, if you don't generate enough sales to cover your "nut," eventually the lights will go off for your business.

The easiest way to calculate your break even is to find the amount of sales at the current gross profit margin that equals the current dollar amount of operating expenses.

Break Even = Fixed Expenses + Interest ÷ Gross Margin

Cash Flow Statements

In addition to your Profit and Loss statements and your Balance Sheet, the third report you should be looking at regularly is your Cash Flow Statement. Your Cash Flow Statement will predict how much cash you have and for how long before you no longer have money to pay the bills.

Remember that profits do not equal cash. Cash is the money you have in hand or coming in the short term to pay bills. Profits may already be spent on taxes, interest, depreciation, long-term debt service, capital purchases, and any number of other items. Cash is king because without it you're out of business. Just like in monopoly, no matter how many hotels you have, if you run out of cash you lose.

Cash Flow Statements can look different, but they should all show the sources of revenue for your business and project out at least ninety, if not 180, days. They should also show debt-service payments and make recommendations as to what to pay and when in order to maximize your money. If you can pay something early to take advantage of a two to three percent discount and you are earning nothing by keeping the money on hand, you should do it. This is the type of money management a good Cash Flow Report will allow you to employ. See the sample cash flow statement at the end of this chapter for an idea of what one might look like.

Twelve Month Trailing Charts

One of the best ways to track data so you can use it in a predictive manner is to use Twelve Month Trailing Charts (often referred to as TTM for total tracked monthly). These allow you to see not only month-to-month trends but also annual trends and to compare the two. A TTM Chart is a rolling annual total that is calculated monthly. Ordinary monthly charts often don't let you know how well you're doing because they only show seasonal or year over year comparisons.

TTM Charts are a fabulous tool because they give you a historical perspective (you can go back as far as you want), while showing a true tend line. Each point on the graph is a total of the previous twelve months, and together they create a very clear picture of how your business is doing and where it is trending. If the line is flat, you're not growing. A downward trend will show even if you had a good month or two. This is a good reality check because, as optimists, we tend to look at the two good months and say things are good. Watching your TTM Chart will allow you to see your company's trends while you still have time to make corrections to your strategy and tactics. Remember what Wayne Gretzky said: "Don't skate to where the puck is, skate to where the puck is going to be."

All of your KPIs should be measured using the TTM trailing methodology. You can also do three, six, and nine month trailing for comparison, but the variability will be greater and this will probably not be as accurate a forecaster. If you doubt the methodology, just compare it to a regular monthly chart and see which one gives you more information.

And please take heart here: anyone who knows a little bit about Excel can create these charts. In his book *CEO Tools: The Nuts-n-Bolts of Business for Every Manager's Success* Kraig Kramers gives very easy to understand, step-by-step instructions for creating your own trailing charts. Incidentally, if your Controller or Accountant can't create these for you, it's time to get a new finance person.

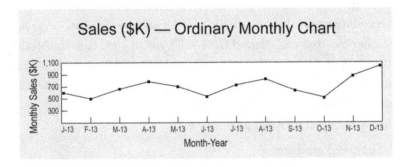

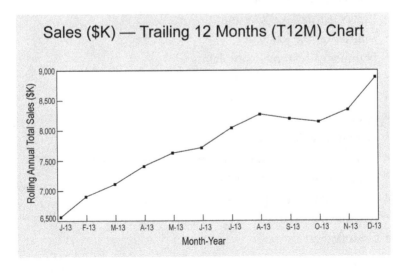

Key Performance Indicators (KPIs)

Like the instruments on your dashboard that tell you how various aspects of your car are functioning, KPIs signal how your business is performing in a particular area. Every business has KPIs, but you have to figure out which ones matter to your business and measure and monitor those over time. Figuring out your most critical, or "leading," KPIs is not always obvious. The way to know if you have chosen the right indicators is to ask these kinds of questions: Does this tell me what's going to happen over the next few months? Does it show me trends? In concert with your Financial Key Indicators, your leading KPIs should show you the direction your business is headed.

Leading Key Performance Indicators are the most important ones for you to track because they help you understand your present and predict your future. There are likely to be a few that are key in your industry. You can do some basic research on your own to find out what these are, and your accountant or investors should also be able to give you suggestions. Remember too that each department will have its own departmental Key Indicators in addition to the company-wide Key Indicators. In thinking through your KPIs you may discover many that apply, but three to five should stand out as most important to your business.

Some examples of KPIs are:

- Returned products
- Scrap on a production line
- Errors per day, week, or month
- Injuries on the job
- Number of customer complaints
- On time vs. late shipments
- Time to delivery of product or service
- Redos
- Sales of new products during first twelve months
- Number of new products delivered to market each year
- Cost of new product development
- New products in top ten markets annually
- Accounts receivable
- Cash flow

- Customer satisfaction
- Dollars per sales representative
- Employee turnover
- Employee morale
- Expenses <%
- Gross Profit per day
- Inventories
- Labor costs compared to sales
- New orders
- Overhead vendor relations
- Productivity
- Utilization
- Working capital
- Book to bill ratio (new bookings to billed out orders or orders shipped)
- Income per employee
- Twelve month rolling ROA
- Month end inventory
- Backlog
- New accounts
- New stores opened
- Same store sales (year to year)
- Number of active customers
- Bid list
- Dollar volume of quotes
- Percent of success of bids
- Labor percent of product cost
- Write downs
- Working capital dollars and ratios
- Line of credit and line drawn
- AR over sixty days and average/day

See the end of this chapter for a sample form you can use to track which KPIs are most important for your company.

Once you've identified your KPIs, it's important to measure them over time and against a specific goal for that period. Also keep in mind that your KPIs are not static. You'll want to revisit which KPIs are giving you the information you need to make the best decisions to grow your business. Sometimes you'll find that a KPI doesn't actually tell you much or that it's redundant. If this is the case, ditch it and find a better indicator. Also, your KPIs can change as your business strategy changes. For instance, if you're having customer service issues, you might develop a more customer-centric approach to your Key Indicators. If you're focused on product development, you might have more key indicators around research and development or time to market for new products. So plan to revisit this exercise periodically. Your KPIs won't do you any good as a strategic tool if they're not measuring what's currently relevant to your company.

Budgets

Finally, you need to think about how you'll approach the budgeting process. Budgeting is essential because your budget is the roadmap that will help you get where you're going while tracking your progress along the way. A bank will not loan you money, nor should they, without a reasonably accurate forecast for the future.

To start, look at what you accomplished last year and project the growth rate you anticipate for the future. Your cost of goods, or selling costs, will rise proportionately as they are a percentage of sales. However, not all of your fixed expenses go up as a function of sales, so make sure you really understand how your expenses are likely to be affected by growth in sales. Again, if your accounting person cannot do this for you accurately, it's time to make a change.

Once you have your budget for the coming fiscal period, move the forecasts up and down to see what effect that has on your business. For instance, if you bring on some key people earlier, will that have a greater impact on sales than waiting and investing in infrastructure? Remember that the most successful businesses are the ones that best predict the future. Your budgets should be the most accurate predictions you can make, not wishful thinking. A good budget makes predicting easier.

Your budget is one of the key instruments on your Dashboard, so pay attention to what it's telling you. Most companies track budget to actual performance on a monthly basis. This allows you to change direction early on if something is not tracking as you anticipated. Although I recommend keeping the budget for the fiscal period set in stone, I do recommend changing the "forecast" every quarter, or a couple of times a year, based on what's actually happening. This allows you to see how you have done against your original predictions and also to make course corrections as needed.

Creating Your Dashboard

Now that you've gotten a sense of the financial tracking tools available to you, learned how to identify your company's KPIs, and thought about a budget, it's time to pull it all together into a "dashboard" that works for your organization. To start, you'll want to identify which financial indicators you need to track regularly (monthly, quarterly, annually) and which KPIs are most important for your business. For the CEO Dashboard, you should only have five or six indicators that you look at daily, weekly, or monthly. Aside from sales and profit, you'll likely want to measure something that is key to your company's strategic objectives for the next couple of years. If one of your objectives is to launch products more quickly, you'll likely want to track time to market or number of new products to market. If you want to grow your business geographically, then you might want to track sales in new territories. If your business is a referral-based business then new referral sources will probably be a good key indicator. Literally, there are hundreds of things you could track; the key is to find the most measurable and predictive for your business, right now. Success is about having the right dashboard, the right indicators for your model of car.

Once you have your dashboard created, what next? Share! You don't need to bring everyone in, but at least your executive team or your management team should be involved. They should all know what their departmental key indicators are and how to manage them. Most companies that use dashboards effectively meet at least monthly, if not bimonthly to share the data. These financial check ins should take no more than thirty minutes, as everyone should know how to read the reports. The purpose of the meeting is simply to discuss course corrections or confirm that the strategy is on track. Once the team gets good at this, it might only take fifteen minutes for everyone to gain a good understanding of the company's health and what they can do to make improvements.

Preventing Fraud

Preventing fraud in your business is about making sure you have the right procedures in place. Always have multiple eyes on critical accounts, regardless of how big or small you are. Every day there are news stories about fraud at companies, regardless of size. Invariably, the fraud occurred because the checks and balances needed to prevent it were not in place. For example, a controller who writes all the checks and balances the bank statements can hide fraud. Not having separate functions for AP and AR can also open you up to fraud.

A CEO I worked with got a call one day from his credit card company. They wanted to know why so many refunds were going into a particular account. They were concerned because, historically, the company hardly ever did refunds. Worse yet, they had called multiple times, but had not been put through to the CEO. As it turned out, his assistant was processing refunds directly into her debit account. Over a two-year period, she deposited $200,000. The bank was only able to get through to the CEO when it did because the assistant happened to be out that day.

Even if you think you have good processes in place, have an outsider take a look and see if they can find cracks. Check with your accountant about doing an audit on your processes to find out where you are vulnerable and fix it. And, above all, do criminal background checks on anyone in finance. You just don't want to make it easy for employees to steal.

Open Book Management (OBM)

Open book management is the practice of teaching all your employees about financial management and how they can impact the company's financial picture. Some very large companies, Whole Foods for one, use this as a practice. Educating your employees about basic business finances can be beneficial to your employees and reap large rewards to your financial bottom line.

The big caveat here is that open book management must be done carefully and well. Remember that most people don't understand business finances and everyone carries their own personal beliefs about money. This combination of ignorance and opinion can be lethal if open book management is not implemented very carefully.

As a cautionary tale, we tried this in my company with very limited success. We had fifty employees and went about putting together a basic financial management class (it was quite similar in concept and material to this chapter). We split the participants into groups of ten, then conducted several classes over the course of six weeks to cover all the topics. The goal was to have the employees understand how the basic finances worked and how their job performance impacted the bottom line both positively and negatively.

Along with the education piece, we implemented a bonus structure (common with OBM), and gave everyone the goals of growing the business and making more money. We did grow and we did make more money, but not as much as my partner wanted and we missed one of the targets. So, rather than giving the employees the partial bonus they had earned, my partner decided we should give them nothing. I was a forty percent owner and, although I strongly disagreed as I felt that denying the partial bonus would undo all the work we had done, we didn't give out the bonus (the peril of minority ownership). As you might imagine, this had a very damaging effect on morale with the result that everyone felt OBM was a joke and that we were greedy owners. The negative fallout of this snowballed to all kinds of judgments about how we were running the business. The purpose of the OBM was to encourage employees to work together as teammates and partners in the business. Clearly we did not accomplish that.

Another conundrum I've seen at smaller businesses that use OBM is deciding exactly what information you want to make open. Do you want your employees to know salaries? What about discretionary expenses? Probably not.

If you decide to implement OBM, you need to decide up front:

- What will you make open?
- What will not be open?
- What are your goals for the project?
- Who will get trained and who will do the training?
- What will the bonus be?
- Will this be a project or an ongoing way of doing business?
- What are your expectations as an owner?
- If you have a board, what are its expectations?

Personally, after my experience, I would not recommend total OBM, but I do think that providing some basic financial knowledge about how the company works is a very good idea. With some basic financial understanding your employees really can help achieve the company's goals.

Financing

Getting a business loan is easy—if you already have all the money you need. If you don't, it can be next to impossible. This is why I tell all my clients, and anyone who will listen: borrow money when you don't need it, when the business is doing well. If you don't actually borrow, at least open up lines of credit you can tap into when you need to because the money will not be available when you need it most.

You only have to go as far back as the great recession of 2008 for proof. Great companies went out of business because banks would not lend them money, regardless of how long they'd been a good client. One large architectural firm was almost forced out of business because its original bank went under. No other bank would take the company in spite of the fact that they made money, had a huge book of business, and, by all banking standards, were a great customer. The firm was finally able to find a bank after being turned down by five, and only after their accounting firm intervened on their behalf. The ratios the new bank required were higher than normal and the interest rate wasn't great, but the company had no choice. Even though all the defaults were in real estate, small businesses took the brunt of those bad lending decisions. Those businesses that had stored up cash, or had quick access to it, were the winners.

There are also banks or hard moneylenders that essentially buy your receivables and pay you in advance. They take a large cut, and I absolutely do not recommend taking this route if it's at all possible to avoid. Doing this is like borrowing from a loan shark because the interest rate grows over time and you end up further in debt than when you started.

If you decide you need to take on debt, how much will depend on three things: your risk tolerance, your credit worthiness, and your business strategy. Know exactly what each of those is, and you'll make the right decisions when it comes to financing for your business.

Not to be overly blunt, but not understanding the concepts outlined in this chapter really amounts to business malpractice. If your financial person doesn't understand them, get someone who does. You do not need to know how to calculate the formulas or the reports I've outlined. But you do need to understand them so you can ask the right questions and make sound decisions. You'll never be able to accomplish your company's intentional purpose without an accurate dashboard that you read often. But, armed with your dashboard, you are far ahead of many entrepreneurial companies. Use this information to your benefit because, the sooner you know where your business is headed, the sooner you'll be able to make course corrections and take advantage of opportunities.

Additional Resources

Key Indicator Summary

Name _____

Company _____

Date _____

Key Indicator	Year		
	20__	20__	20__ Adjusted YTD Rolling Average
Profit/Loss Indicators			
Revenue			
Cost of Sales			
Expenses			
Profit			
Cash Flow Indicators			
Accounts Receivable			
Accounts Payable			
Bank Line Tap			
Working Capital			
Inventory			
Operational Indicators			
Backlog			
Bid List			
% Success on Bids			
# of Competitors			
Market Share			
Liquidity Ratio			
Sales Indicators			
$/Rep.			
New Orders/Rep.			
# of Active Customers			
Appt./Close Rate			
Labor Costs to Sales			
Customer Satisfaction Indicators			
% On-Time Delivers			
Volume by Customer			
Turnover Rate			
Error Rate			
Returns/Rejects			
Complaints			
Productivity Indicators			
Hours/Project			
Customer Profitability			

Cash Flow Statement

	For the Year Ending	12/31/11
	Cash at Beginning of Year	15,700

Operations
Cash receipts from customers	693,200
Cash paid for	
Inventory purchases	(264,000)
General operating and administrative expenses	(112,000)
Wage expenses	(123,000)
Interest	(13,500)
Income taxes	(32,800)
Net Cash Flow from Operations	**147,900**

Investing Activities
Cash receipts from	
Sale of property and equipment	33,600
Collection of principal on loans	
Sale of investment securities	
Cash paid for	
Purchase of property and equipment	(75,000)
Making loans to other entities	
Purchase of invesment securities	
Net Cash Flow from Investing Activities	**(41,400)**

Financing Activities
Cash receipts from	
Issuance of stock	
Borrowing	
Cash paid for	
Repurchase of stock (treasury stock)	
Repayment of loans	(34,000)
Dividends	(53,000)
Net Increase in Cash	**(87,000)**
	19,500

	Cash at End of Year	35,200

Financial Dashboard Checklist

- ❏ Identify the five to six most important Key Financial Indicators for your company.

- ❏ Decide which metrics you will track on your twelve month trailing charts.

- ❏ Identify the most important Key Performance Indicators for your company.

- ❏ Decide what your budgeting process will be.

- ❏ Describe how you will you make sure your executive team understands the Dashboard for the company.

- ❏ List where you think you might be vulnerable to fraud.

- ❏ Decide what you will change to safeguard against fraud.

- ❏ Decide what financing methods you will employ.

Recommended Reading

CEO Tools: The Nuts-n-Bolts of Business for every Manager's Success, Kraig Kramers, Gandy Dancer Press, 2002.

Make Your Move: Change the Way You Look At Your Business and Increase Your Bottom Line, Alan and Brian Beaulieu, Morgan James Publishing, 2010.

Managing By The Numbers: A Complete Guide to Understanding And Using Your Company's Financials, Chuck Kremer, Ron Rizzuto, and John Case, Basic Books, 2000.

Puzzle Piece Nine
Strategy +
Operations =
Execution

Entrepreneurs are sometimes famous for having brilliant ideas without a lot of follow-through. Another way of saying this is that a lot of entrepreneurial enterprises lack the operational capacity to execute. That's why I contend that Strategy + Operations = Execution. And without execution your business just cannot operate.

Here are a few statistics on the probability of completing a goal from the American Society of Training and Development:

- Hear an idea: 10%
- Consciously decide to adopt it: 25%
- Decide when you'll do it: 40%
- Plan how you'll do it: 50%
- Commit to someone else that you'll do it: 65%
- Have a specific accountability appointment with the person committed to: 95%

So clearly it's essential to have an actual process for implementing and following through on your business goals, and that's what this chapter will focus on.

Think of goals as *what* you are going to do, and strategy as *how* you are going to do it. Operations is responsible for acting on the strategy, or delivering on the goals. Entrepreneur, Alice Cunningham, owner of Olympic Hot Tub and Spa, says there are three keys to running a successful business: making a product easy to buy, easy to own, and easy to refer. Strategy dictates how to achieve these goals, while operations makes it happen. Assuming you have your vision and values defined as outlined in Chapter One, let's focus on how to actually get things done.

Strategic Priorities

Let's start by clarifying a few terms. You've no doubt heard a lot of words associated with the idea of a strategic plan: strategic initiatives, goals, vision, tactics, actions, objectives, and probably many more. Let's simplify all of this by visualizing this as a series of ripples in a pond, where each individual ripple's energy drives the next one out in the ring so that, while they might appear separate, each one creates movement in the next:

Values are the first drop of water that creates and drives each subsequent ripple as it moves outward.

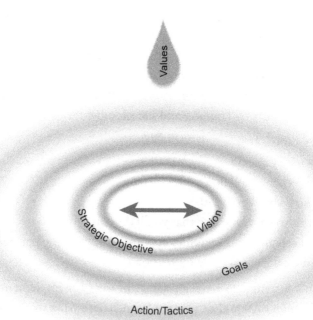

Vision is the next ripple out. Vision is your overarching purpose; the thing you're trying to accomplish; the place your business will be in three to five years.

Strategic Initiative (or Objective) is a focus area that needs action or change over a period of time for the vision to be achieved. The time frame can be more than a year, and you'll likely have only three to four strategic initiatives at a time, as more than that will be difficult to execute.

Goals are very specific things that need to happen within any strategic initiative. Each goal should adhere to the SMART principle:

- **S**pecific: It's clearly defined, with actions and individuals named to achieve it.
- **M**easurable: There is some way to quantify if you've accomplished it.
- **A**chievable: It can actually be achieved.
- **R**esults Based: There is a tangible result associated with it.
- **T**ime Bound: There are specific time-based benchmarks for accomplishment of the goal.

Actions/Tactics are the specific steps that need to happen for each goal in order to accomplish the overall objectives and therefore the vision. Actions are not goals; they are *how* you'll accomplish each goal.

Take a soccer team, for example. The coach's vision might be to take his team to nationals. His strategic objectives might include winning the regional title, creating a name for the team regionally and nationally, and creating a team of world-class players. His goal to achieve this might be to win X number of games during the season. The actions or tactics to do this might be to have a practice schedule to train players, recruit new players, and score goals during each game.

The operations team of any company has to execute on the actions and tactics in order to deliver on the goals so that they can achieve the strategic objectives and ultimately the vision. In order for them to be able to do all that, the executives need to provide a clear vision, which is why you did all the work you did in Chapter One. Without a clear—and clearly communicated—vision the actions and tactics your operations team is supposed to implement won't make sense.

I'm sure you've heard lots of stories of companies doing something because "that's the way it's always been done." That happens because, somewhere along the line, the vision changed or was not shared so the actions didn't have meaning. This can also happen when a strategic initiative is achieved, but its success is not communicated. When either of these things happens, people end up disliking their actions because they aren't meaningful. The result is a loss of both human and financial resources.

A distributor of metal products had always created a catalog of all of their products to send out to their clients. The catalogues were very expensive and time consuming to produce, and everyone in operations believed the customers really didn't read them anymore because all that information was available online. The print catalogue had long since served its purpose, but no one at the executive level was listening. Had they thought about the print catalogue in terms of whether or not it was serving the vision—and consequently the strategic objectives—they would have stopped producing it and spent the resources elsewhere. And, had the CEO enabled operations to bring this issue up in a constructive way, the issue might have been addressed sooner. So remember, operations knows a lot more than you might think they do and when you give them vision, purpose, and direction they'll do marvelous things for your company.

Outlining the Plan

Strategic planning is nothing more than developing or fine-tuning the plan that will achieve your vision in a given amount of time. You should define three to four strategic objectives (your most important priorities), and two to three goals per strategic objective with multiple tactics for each goal. You can begin your thinking process by asking yourself some questions:

- What are the three things I have to accomplish in the next six months?
- Do they support my vision?
- What strategic objective do they support?
- What goals and actions or tactics need to be executed to keep things on plan?

When it comes to actually having your strategic planning session, however, I recommend using an outside facilitator. You and your team are likely too close to your plans to be objective—you won't be able to identify gaps in your thinking or see future opportunities. A qualified facilitator will help you see these things while reaching a consensus efficiently. And, when you don't have to be the leader for a while, you can participate more fully.

Your Operations Team

These are the folks who make your business happen. In each company operations looks a little different. Sometimes it's production, sometimes it's finance, sometimes it's creative, sometimes it's scheduling or customer service. But in any company, at its most basic, operations is simply the folks who make it happen. So, who in your company do you consider part of your operations team?

Identifying Interested Parties

One of the biggest difficulties in organizations is not recognizing who might be affected by your initiatives. The "theory of constraints" says that every time you fix a problem or bottleneck, another one will appear somewhere else. The smallest change to production or engineering can have a huge ripple effect on operations. Change can be particularly problematic in small companies where the downstream effects are not well thought out. The advantage of being small is that it allows organizations to be nimble, making changes quickly. But the downside of this is that one ill-conceived change can cause huge bottlenecks.

The bottom line is, no matter how large or small your company, think through both the operational change and who needs to know about it *before* you implement. This is not the time to fire from the hip. Notifying all the interested parties before an operational change takes place is also a good time to encourage input. Your downstream employees might have some real insight into the possible effects of a change initiative, potentially saving you a real headache. This is an area where being proactive keeps employees happy and systems moving forward.

Communication Plan

Develop clear language and a plan to communicate your strategic initiatives to your employees. Make sure your people understand your expectations. Be transparent about your goals and the time frame for achieving them. Remember, when people don't get information from you, they'll make up stories to explain what's happening. Stories get retold and become facts, and before long your company is marching to a drum you're not playing. So, take control before the change starts! Decide how to communicate what you want accomplished. Tell people how it will be measured, and how you will tell them when they've succeeded (verbally, in the company newsletter, via email, etc.).

Developing the Action Plan

Take a look at your strategic objectives and make a plan. Your plan should include clear goals and the actions needed to accomplish them. Those actions should be delegated to the appropriate people with a time frame for completion. Use the chart at the end of this chapter for each of the goals you're trying to achieve and list as many actions as need to take place on each. Get input from your operations team and together determine if you can meet each of these goals within the time frame.

Debrief Model

The mark of any successful company is the ability to learn from everything they do. Although most of us would rather hide and pretend we didn't create some of the debacles we call business initiatives, if you're open you have much to learn from your own mistakes and those of others. I cannot emphasize enough how important it is to have these conversations and not avoid them. The basic idea is to go through what went well, what didn't go so well, and what changes you would make as a result. Doing this is called "debriefing" (sometimes also an "oil change" or, more recently, the Agile method), and it's the one step in the strategic initiative process that will keep you ahead of your competitors and on track to achieve your plans.

Having a model to follow will help you conduct a productive conversation. I like the one from Conversant at the end of this chapter because it incorporates all aspects of a debrief. Use it in your company regularly and you'll encourage valuable conversations that will lead to happier and more productive employees. Create a culture of conversation and you won't be creating catalogs no one wants!

Additional Resources

Individual Goals Worksheet

Individual Goals Worksheet

Name _____   Date _____

20__ Goals
Personal & Professional Development Plan

3-5 Year Strategic Vision:

Values:

Strategic Objectives (3 business, 1 personal)	20__ Business Goals
20__ Professional Development Goals	20__ Personal Goals (family, wealth, wellness, recreation)

Best decision of 20__:

Worst decision of 20__:

The Standard Conversational Debrief

Reprinted with permission from The Communication Catalyst *by Mickey Connolly & Richard Rianoshek, Ph.D., 2002.*

In the *act* of conversations, we set the stage for accountability. Adjustment is the true test of accountability, host frequent debriefs of performance. Have the debriefing sessions be open, public conversations including all significant stakeholders. Initially, many people balk at public debriefing because of the threat of embarrassment. High-velocity value requires the system of interests to debrief and adjust together. Personal discomfort must be junior to the acceleration of value.

Stage One: Review

State the original purpose and any specific results that were promised. If the first step is difficult, you have your first lesson: you were never aligned regarding purpose.

State the accurate outcome to date. Separate facts and explanations. Only accept mutually agreed facts. Treat facts under dispute like explanations.

What worked well in achieving the purpose and the promised results? What were valuable insights, methods, and mindsets? Sort the input into the cycle of value conversations: align (intersect, invent, invest), act (engage, clarify, close), and adjust (review, renew).

What worked poorly since the last review? Acknowledge goals unmet, disappointments, and mistakes of commission and omission. Sort the input into the conversations: align (intersect, invent, invest), act (engage, clarify, close), and adjust (review, renew).

Who is there to appreciate? Who specifically? What specifically did they provide? How and when will you recognize them?

Stage Two: Renew

What actionable lessons will produce value going forward? How will what you learned change how you act? What new action(s) will you take immediately? Share the lessons with whoever will benefit.

What area of improvement is our highest priority focus? What cycle of value conversation is it in? Is it an issue of insight (information, analysis, concepts), method (skills, processes), and/or self (mindsets, personal patterns)? What structures and measures are needed to support adjustments?

Debrief Worksheet

1. State the original purpose and/or goals.

2. State the actual outcome to date. (Separate what actually happened from comments, interpretations, etc. regarding what actually happened.)

3. What worked well regarding the original purpose and/or goals?

4. What goals were met or exceeded?

5. What methods were successful?

6. What did not work well?

7. What did not work well regarding the original purpose and/or goals?

8. What goals were not met?

9. What was disappointing?

10. What were the mistakes of commission or omission?

11. What was missing?

12. Who deserves appreciation?

13. What specifically did they provide?

14. How and when will you recognize them?

15. What did we learn that will benefit us now and in the future?

16. How will what we learned change how we act in the future?

17. What area of competence is weak or missing that would make a high-leverage difference in our work?

18. Share what was learned with whomever will benefit.

Strategic Initiatives Checklist

❒ List the three initiatives you must accomplish in the next six months.

❒ Describe how they support your vision.

❒ Describe the strategic objectives they support.

❒ List your goals for each initiative.

❒ List the actions/tactics necessary to complete each goal.

❒ List the members of your Operations Team.

❒ List the interested parties.

❒ Develop a communication plan.

❒ Select an outside facilitator for the strategic planning session.

❒ Debrief after the each initiative has been achieved.

Recommended Reading

Execution: The Discipline of Getting Things Done, Larry Bossidy, Ram Charan, Charles Burck, Random House Business Books, 2011.

The Communication Catalyst, Mickey Connolly and Richard Rianoshek, Ph.D., Kaplan Publishing, 2001.

The E-Myth Revisited: Why Most Small Businesses Don't Work and What to Do About It, Michael Gerber, HarperCollins, 1995.

Puzzle Piece Ten
Exit Strategy

If you don't start with the end in mind, the end usually comes as a big surprise and, generally speaking, it *won't* be what you had in mind. The first question a venture capitalist will ask when evaluating a potential business or idea is, "What's the end game?" What they're really looking for is a significant opportunity to leverage capital to maximize the return on their money, building shareholder value for themselves and their investors. They're looking for the greatest return on their investment dollars in the shortest amount of time.

Why should you be any different? Presumably, you're investing startup capital in your business that could be used for a different investment vehicle, so evaluate this investment as you would any holding in your portfolio. Yes, it offers benefits such as allowing you to be your own boss and launch your own ideas, but it is, at its most basic, an investment, so treat it as one.

When Do You Want To Be Done Working?

Creating an exit strategy starts with answering a simple question: when do you want to be done? I've heard many responses to this and one of the most common is: "Well, if the price were right, I could be done tomorrow." Clearly that's not a realistic answer for planning purposes. Another common response people give is that they'll stop working when they reach a particular age, usually sixty or sixty-five. But again, that doesn't address the issue of what *you* will do to create your retirement circumstances. What will your life and business look like when you're ready to leave? The reality is, most of the time, what people really mean is that they don't really know. For some entrepreneurs, talking about retirement is about as comfortable as talking about death.

Nonetheless, what you want your retirement to look like is an important topic because it will guide the decisions you make for your business. If you start your business at forty-five and want to work until you're sixty (and you mean it), you have fifteen years to maximize the investment in your business. On the other hand, if you start at thirty with the same retirement goal, thirty years probably allows you to take more risks and possibly move the business in a different direction than you would with a shorter time frame.

Maybe your exit plan is to leave *this* business, but not to retire. Serial entrepreneurs just keep creating new businesses because they can't help themselves. One very smart CEO I work with is on his tenth or eleventh business. He keeps saying he'll retire someday, but we both know he won't. Whether you want to retire or move onto another business, however, you still need an exit plan.

What Would You Be Doing if You Didn't Have Your Business?

Take some time to think about when you no longer wish to be working in *any* business. Make a list of all the things you want to do when you're no longer working. If it's not a very long list, you probably want to be "working" a lot longer than you think, maybe just in a different capacity. If you're really struggling with this exercise, I suggest taking a retreat by yourself or with your partner and spend several days just thinking about it. Commit to having an answer by the end of your retreat. Without all the clutter of your daily life, you should be able to picture your future more clearly.

I often work with CEOs who want to stop working or are ready to sell, but they don't know what they'll do when that happens. So they just keep doing what they know how to do, sometimes missing the best opportunity to sell the company. Selling your company is an *emotional* decision, not just a financial one. A software company CEO knew intellectually that it was the right time to sell. He'd had several inquiries from large companies, but couldn't seem to sign the papers for the investment firm to represent him. After a lot of hard, very emotional questions, we discovered that he had no idea what to do with himself if and when his company did sell. This frightened him to the point of inaction—so much so that he was potentially missing an opportunity to cash in on what he'd built. We explored the options he had and decided that he would take about a year off and start another company. Doing this gave him peace of mind and a sense of purpose, and allowed him to let go of the current business.

Sometimes the answer to the above question is, "I'd have another business that didn't have all these issues." I have news for you: all businesses have issues. So you can work to solve the problems at yours and capitalize on your investment or sell it and start over. Either is a good option, just know what you want and why you're doing it as that will color your choices. You can't hide from yourself, so be honest.

There are no right or wrong answers here, just the ones that are right for you. The point is to be intentional so you can plan for your own future in the process of running your business. And be sure to revisit your retirement plan every few years, as your thinking is likely to change.

How Much Do You Want In the Bank After the Sale?

Let me just preface this discussion by stressing that you should really use a financial advisor to help you determine this number. This is the number that will allow you to start a new business, or maintain the lifestyle of your choice while never working again. In all likelihood not all of your retirement money will come from selling your business—you probably have other assets or investments—but certainly you are expecting some end profit from this investment, the ROI on your business. How much you need to sell your business for can be complicated to figure out because what you walk away with depends so much on things like your tax structure and the estate planning you do prior to selling.

You'll want to spend some time contemplating what you want life after *this* business to look like (whether that's starting another business or retiring), and what you need to do now to make that happen. Include your spouse or partner. Talk to your financial advisor. Then, as I said before, reevaluate your plan regularly to make sure it still accurately reflects your lifestyle goals as well the inevitable surprises that come up.

Current Assessment of Business Value

You really do need an expert to help you determine the value of your company and, as a rule, I recommend an evaluation at least every three years, if not every other year. When I worked in mergers and acquisitions for smaller firms, the business owner was almost always surprised by the valuation. The value was never *more* than they expected. Although I've just said that selling your business is an emotional decision, try to be as objective as you can. Potential buyers don't share your emotional investment. You won't get paid back for all the blood, sweat, and tears you put in over the years. You won't get paid back for your anguish over all the risks you took. You *will* get paid for value: the financial value the business has to investors to operate as a sustainable enterprise, or the strategic value it brings to another firm.

Following is a quick breakdown of the various valuation methodologies in the most basic terms.

Balance Sheet Based
- Book Value = Balance sheet assets – liabilities
- Liquidation Value = Discounted balance sheet assets – liabilities
- Fair Market Value = Fair market value of your assets – liabilities

Earnings Based
- **EBIT and EBITDA Multiples** = Multiples-based net earnings + addbacks for owner salaries, taxes, interest, and any other benefits defined as tied to current owners or ownership structure (EBIT). EBITDA simply adds depreciation and amortization to that calculation.
- **Discounted Cash Flow** is a valuation based on cash flow, discounted for a variety of factors.
- **Capitalization of Earnings** (earnings cap method): According to Wikipedia this is "an income-valuation approach that determines

the value of a business by looking at the current benefit of realizing a cash flow now, rather than in the future."

Market Based

- **Earnings Multiple:** Some multiple of earnings, for example two times revenue or five times EBITDA.
- **Industry Rule of Thumb:** Whatever the standard is for your industry: e.g., financial services firms typically go for three to five times earnings over a certain level.

Buyer's Feasibility

- **Cash Flow Adequacy:** Can the business pay for itself? Is there sufficient cash flow to cover the debt service of the purchase?
- **Payback Period:** How long it will take to pay off the purchase price from earnings.
- **Return on Investment (ROI):** The rate of return for the capital investment someone would be making in the business.

Which method you use is really dependent on the reason for the evaluation. For instance, when I bought into a company I was working for, we had a shareholder evaluation done, which is typically lower than a market-based evaluation. A shareholder evaluation is done when you're giving or selling shares to family members or internal employees you might want to incentivize with future earning potential.

When selling to outside investors, you'll most likely have a combination of earnings-based and market-based methods. A savvy investment banker will have a good idea of what the multiple is for your industry. And that person should also be able to tell you what that number would be if your company were X size. It's often advantageous to keep your business and grow it just a little more to capitalize on your investment.

Current S.W.O.T.

What are your company's Strengths, Weaknesses, Opportunities, and Threats? Although you should be doing this annually to take advantage of or protect market positions, when doing this with a sale in mind, you'll know what your ideal ROI is (I'll call this your "number"). This will advance different conversations based on your number and time frame. What will best maximize what you currently have? What does this tell you about when to sell? Is that sooner or later than you had planned?

Examine your strategic position in the marketplace. This will tell you a lot about who might want to buy your company, and what you could do to enhance its value. This might include making a purchase yourself to create a succession plan for the business, or to enhance its value to get you closer to your number.

Exit Options

You always have multiple options for exit, they're just valued differently, so your decisions will be different based on your number and the legacy you want for your business. As you think about all this, also keep in mind that a business should be sold when it's doing well, not when it's on the down slope of the business cycle. That's where your exit plan will serve you well. And don't forget that it's also an option not to exit.

Strategic Buyer vs. Traditional Buyer

You won't have much argument that in most cases a strategic sale is worth more to you than a traditional buyer. Strategic buyers are those who can exponentially increase the value of their company by purchasing yours. Rollups were popular in the nineties as a way of maximizing value for all parties involved. A manufacturer would buy up the distributors in the industry or the logistics handler to control all aspects of the business and have an edge over the competition. A strategic buyer will often pay a premium for your business because it's worth it to them. Microsoft has made hundreds of "strategic buys" in the tech world because, in some cases, it's cheaper to buy a product than create it. In most cases a strategic buyer is also purchasing your market share.

Family Sale

Keeping the business in the family or selling to family members can be a good option. At least for a while. Think about the generational businesses you know. Often, the first generation is entrepreneurial: they have big ideas, they're engaging, and they get something started that didn't exist before. The second generation comes along and sometimes there's a good manager in the bunch. That person has had good training by the founder, and there's a solid succession plan in place. However, by the third generation, a sense of entitlement may have crept in, eroding the founder's work ethic. Think about Nordstrom or Walmart. By the third generation, Nordstrom's second generation had to come out of retirement to set things right again. Sam Walton is probably turning in his grave at some of the waste his heirs have created.

If you're going to keep the business in the family and sell it to children or other family members, you should work with a family business specialist who can help you through the exit planning with all the complexities families create. They can help you plan, train for, and execute a transition strategy that can save the business for your family and generations to come, and that leaves you with what you need. Even though you're dealing with family, think of this like any other business transaction and don't compromise to accommodate a family member's shortcomings. If you wouldn't concede something for an outside investor, you probably shouldn't do it for an inside investor, even your kids. Most importantly, make everything visible, talk about expectations, and have a plan for what to do if things don't go as intended.

Employee Stock Ownership Plan (ESOP)

An ESOP is a sale to your employees. You arrange a stock value and sell shares to your employees or a group of employees, or they can earn shares as part of their compensation. I've seen as many unsuccessful ESOPs as successful ones. One owner sold a portion of his business to his employees in an ESOP transaction. The owner still had a significant stake in the business (sixty percent) as the transaction was playing out. At that point a strategic buyer made an offer that was approximately four times the ESOP valuation. Although the employees would all have made a significant return on their investment (the owner had kept share values low, gifted shares, and allowed employees to earn shares as bonuses), they refused to approve the outside sale, which was their right according to the ESOP rules. The owner was furious, but there was nothing he could do because the new leadership felt they didn't want or need to sell. Consequently, the owner spent the next two years and several hundred thousand dollars in attorney's fees rescinding the ESOP. He finally won, but the end result was the departure of many key employees, lost business, bitter feelings, and no interest from buyers. (ESOPs can also be risky for employees, especially if they're buying in with their 401K or retirement. If the company folds, they're left with nothing and they're out of a job.)

But I have seen successful ESOPs as well, where the employees took ownership, felt empowered, and increased the value of the company. The lesson here is to be very careful, specific, and clear about all eventualities with an ESOP. Be sure to get the best legal and accounting advice you can find.

Potential Suitors

As you're thinking about your exit from your business, it's good to start and keep a list of potential suitors. These are individuals who have expressed interest in the past, as well as potential strategic buyers for whom your business would be a jewel. Once you have the list, check in with these people to keep your company on their radar. The best business deals are not made when the owner decides to sell; they are made long before by cultivating partnerships and relationships that might one day bear fruit. This does not mean you have a perpetual "for sale" sign up for your business. Rather, it means that you are always ready for an opportunity should one present at the right time and for the right price.

Transition Team

Your team will include a group of professionals who know exactly what to do when a change happens, be it planned or unplanned. The team members should include your accounting firm, business attorney, estate attorney, board members or advisors, insurance advisor, mentor, investment analyst/advisor or broker, and any high-level members of the management team. The reason to include most of these professionals might be obvious, but I'll discuss them anyway because this aspect of planning is so important.

- **Accounting Firm** Your accountant should have an up-to-date picture of all the company's financial and tax information, as well as the current business valuation. Your accountant will be counted on for tax advice as it relates to the transition or sale and as well as for maximizing value for owners, heirs, or employees.

- **Business Attorney** The company's business attorney should have a copy of the transition plan, and assist with execution in the event of a founder death or incapacity. This person should have a list of the team and be able to act as executor if needed.

- **Estate Attorney** The estate attorney will be the one who has set things up in advance in trusts or other vehicles so that, again, no undo tax is paid or owed as a result of poor planning. This person should be directed by the founders as to specific requests in the event of any type of liquidity event or unforeseen occurrence.

- **Board Members or Advisors** This group needs to be involved if they are stepping in for a departed founder or leader, or if they are advising on a sale.

- **Mentor** This person usually will have had the ear of the owner/founder/CEO and can help execute any plan that's put into place. This person can sometimes act as an interim, depending on qualifications.

- **Insurance Advisor** This person will need to be brought in if any key man insurance was purchased and needs to be exercised.

- **Investment Analyst/Advisor** This advisor will be brought in to do the valuation or update an existing one, and to find or negotiate with the buyer or buyers.

- **Management Team** Only senior executives need to be a part of this team as it relates to what roles they play in any transition. However, they should all be aware of what the plan is for any event.

The Succession Plan

Just in case you're still wondering if you need one, let me give you an example of what can happen if you don't think this through now. A manufacturing business I worked with was a family company that had a proprietary product in the construction industry. Although the revenues were upwards of $150 million, the founder's eighty year-old wife did the books by hand. And I do mean by hand—she refused to use a computer and actually still used the old ledger books instead. Over sixty years of operating the business they had had multiple offers to buy, but never gave them any attention. The founder refused to give his son any real control and never cultivated a management team. One day on the job the eighty-five year-old founder dropped dead of a heart attack. A week later his wife died. The son had no idea what to do and, although the business had no debt, it quickly went down hill without the father to guide things. No one had done any planning for what would happen after the founders were gone, and the son was completely unprepared. Although the books were accurate, because they were done by hand, no buyer would believe it, much less pay top dollar for the business. The company was eventually sold at a discount for its asset value and one patent. The family received pennies on the dollar for a formerly prosperous business. The plant was shuttered and 150 employees lost their jobs. Although this is an extreme story, I've experienced many others just as sad for the founders, family, or employees. All for lack of a real succession plan.

Now that you have all of the elements and I've convinced you that it's really necessary, it's time to put together your plan. Just as you would have an outside facilitator help you formulate a strategic plan, you should also consider an outside person to help with your succession plan. After all, this is also a strategic plan, just for a different purpose. Make sure you've involved all the appropriate people (see above), and have the plan in writing.

Your plan doesn't need to be long or complicated (although some of the legal and tax implications can be), and you should be able to have it outlined in two to three pages. Each of the team members will likely have a more detailed plan for their roles, but the overall strategy need not be complicated. Your plan might be a fairly simple statement like this: "The business will grow to X dollars, and then we will sell to one of three strategic buyers for X dollars. The following people will make up the transition team." And then you'd go in more detail from there. Be sure to involve your business partners, management team, and family members in the decisions so they know exactly what to do if you're not around to direct the show.

As you are putting together your succession plan, you should put together what I call a Business Plan B Notebook in case something happens to you before you plan to leave. Your Plan B Notebook contains all the key information about the business including accounts, insurance, family contacts, locations of key items and documents, etc. See the Plan B Notebook worksheet at the end of this chapter. Make sure someone knows where your notebook is and keep it updated.

Revisit your succession plan every few years or so to make sure you're still comfortable with it. It's perfectly okay to change your mind, because of course you will depending on what life throws your way. Be flexible, but feel secure knowing that you actually have a plan to keep your most important investment safe.

Additional Resources

Business Plan B Notebook

Purpose: In case of a major emergency there is a plan to take care of the business.

Information

- ❏ Bank (account numbers, passwords, banker)
- ❏ Bookkeeper (all contact information)
- ❏ Accountant (all contact information)
- ❏ Financial Planner/Stockbroker (all contact information)
- ❏ Access points
- ❏ Cell Phone (account number and password)
- ❏ Landline (account number and password)
- ❏ Web site (host information, account number, password)
- ❏ Web person(s) (all contact information)
- ❏ I.T. person (all contact information)
- ❏ Lawyer (all contact information)
- ❏ Executor for business (all contact information)
- ❏ Insurance agent(s) (all contact information)
- ❏ Office/Personal assistants (all contact information)
- ❏ Family Contact info for office assistants (parents, spouse, in-laws, keyholder for home, pet sitter, baby sitter)
- ❏ Safety deposit box location

Documents (list locations and relevant information for each)

- ❏ Bank accounts
- ❏ Business documents (license, corporate shareholders agreements, LLC operating agreement, etc.)
- ❏ Insurance
- ❏ General Commercial Liability
- ❏ Disability
- ❏ Health
- ❏ Life
- ❏ Malpractice/E&O
- ❏ Homeowners
- ❏ Major client contracts
- ❏ List of where to locate physical items like checkbook

- ❏ Renewals (domain names, business license, associations)
- ❏ Credit cards for business
- ❏ Power of attorney
- ❏ Business
- ❏ Healthcare
- ❏ Passwords (computer, applications, etc.): Needs to be in a separate location from this book.
- ❏ Property (residential and commercial, including leases)

Plan B

Who will do what if:

- ❏ Flight delayed many days
- ❏ Serious illness or injury
- ❏ Natural disaster with disrupted communications

Exit Strategy Checklist

- ❏ Set the date when you want to be done working.
- ❏ Describe what you would be doing if you didn't have your business.
- ❏ Determine you number: ascertain how much you want in the bank after the sale.
- ❏ Current Assessment of Business Value:
    - ❏ Who did/will do the assessment?
    - ❏ What type of valuation was/will be done?
    - ❏ Date of valuation:
    - ❏ Amount assessed:
- ❏ Current S.W.O.T.:
    - ❏ Strengths
    - ❏ Weaknesses
    - ❏ Opportunities
    - ❏ Threats
- ❏ List type of exit option in order preference (Sale to outside, family, ESOP or IPO).
- ❏ List potential suitors
- ❏ List transition team:
    - ❏ Accountant
    - ❏ Attorney
    - ❏ Board Members/Advisors
    - ❏ Mentor
    - ❏ Insurance Analyst
    - ❏ Broker/Investment Analyst
    - ❏ Banker
    - ❏ Other
- ❏ Construct Business Plan B Notebook

Recommended Reading

The Number: What Do You Need for the Rest of Your Life and What Will it Cost?, Lee Eisenberg, Free Press, 2006.

Afterword

My wish for you as an entrepreneur is that you give your dreams the chance to happen. Some of the things you try will be successful, some will not, and some will give you opportunities to learn things you never imagined.

As I said at the beginning of this book, begin with the end in mind and you will have a much greater likelihood of achieving the success you desire. This book is filled with tips, tactics, and advice for all of you who are already running your own businesses as well of those of you still dreaming. My hope is that these ten pieces will help you see the big picture of your success and cut down on frustration along the way. So I'll end where I began by reminding you that the pieces are important, but only to the extent they contribute to that big picture, your intentional purpose, because that's what gives meaning to all the day to day stuff you and your employees do.

Spend time on your intentional purpose, live it in your business, and the practicalities will fall into place. I'm not saying it will be easy, but difficulties are tolerable when they have a larger purpose. Being an entrepreneur means working at the edge, experimenting, taking risks, and, yes, failing. But, as long as you learn and remember to have some fun, those failures will bring you closer to a successful business enterprise. I often tell CEOs to remember the Three Fs: Fail Fast and have Fun!

About the Author

Mary E. Marshall is an entrepreneur who has spent her career making small businesses into successful ventures. She has done this both as a CEO and business owner herself, and as an executive coach and consultant. Mary has also worked with Vistage International as a peer coach to CEOs and business executives. While at Vistage, Mary was awarded the Rookie of the Year, Chair Excellence, and Star awards, and received the Master Chair designation. She was consistently ranked among the top Vistage Chairs in the country and was the first woman in Vistage history to hold the #1 Chair ranking for the U.S. In 2012 Mary left corporate life at Vistage to go back to what she loves best: working directly with entrepreneurs to help them achieve their dreams. She launched Marshall Advisors, LLC as an Executive Advisory agency to work with CEOs and their executive teams to help them achieve their goals more quickly and efficiently, and to have some fun while doing it! In addition to her work with business entrepreneurs, Mary also shares her expertise with Social Venture Partners and teaches a class for entrepreneurs at The Small Business Administration. She is currently studying to become certified as a Tribal Leader with author and speaker Dave Logan. Learn more about Marshall Advisors and follow Mary's blog at www.mary-marshall.com.

Index

Page numbers in italics indicate a real life example of the topic. Page numbers with a t indicate a table (e.g. 139t). Hyphenated terms are listed alphabetically as if one word (e.g., pre-tax comes after presentations).